Bending the Bars

John Barker

CHRISTIEBOOKS

HASTINGS

BENDING THE BARS
by John Barker

This edition published in Great Britain in 2006
by ChristieBooks
PO Box 35, Hastings, East Sussex, TN34 2UX
christie@btclick.com
www.tvhastingschristiebooks.com

First limited edition: ChristieBooks, Hastings — 2002
This edition: ChristieBooks, Hastings — 2006

Distributed in the UK by Central Books Ltd
99 Wallis Road, London E9 5LN
orders@centralbooks.com

ISBN 1-873976-31-3

British Library Cataloguing in Publication Data.
A catalogue record for this book is available from the British Library

Barker, John, 1947 -
A catalogue for this book is available from the British Library

ISBN 1-873976-31-3

Contents

This book is an obviously selective memoir of being in maximum security prisons between 1971 and 1978. I went in at 23 and came out at thirty. It was written in the form of stories towards the end of the sentence and finished soon after my release. The impetus for writing came from the stories of 'Brownie' that had started to appear in *Republican News*. Written from inside Long Kesh prison, they had a humanist, political wit to them. Now it is known that Brownie was the pen name of Gerry Adams, and that in retrospect these stories were part of the long haul by Gerry and other Kesh graduates like Gerry Kelly (who makes an appearance in this book) to pull the Irish Republican movement out of the rut of a military-only Catholic nationalism.

My stories have no such significance, nor should they be taken as a picture of how prisons are now. I can say with no laughter that my time inside was the golden age of such prisons. In the 'Labour' chapter a Chief Officer is described as 'a smiler, a relic from the future wherein, it is wrongly assumed, prisons among other things, would become progressively more liberal'. Since that time we have endured Mrs Thatcher, Michael Howard and Tony Blair, all keen on punishing people who are not 'Hard-working families who play by the rules' as Blair put it. Prison is almost exclusively for working class people who do not 'play by the rules'.

The introduction of 'Prison Works', a system of reward and punishment that is both formal and arbitrary pre-dates New Labour but is wholly suited to its authoritarian moralizing. Prison 'privileges' as they are laughingly called are only for those who play by the rules, unwritten rules as to your behaviour, demeanour, your very way of being. In the wider world it is matched by New Labour's No Rights without Responsibilities slogan. As Mark Barnsley (maximum injustice for 8 long years) has described, it is like an experiment in social control for which New Labour no doubt have targets and league tables. Its purpose to destroy what remains of collective solidarity among cons after years of 'Thacherite' individualism and too much heroin. Under New Labour there are even cells under permanent CCTV watch.

At the same time competitively repressive New Labour Home Secretaries have made their own further contributions to worsening conditions. Pile Them High! Perhaps it is their fanatical pro-Americanism that wants them to match US imprisonment rates. But with ever rising numbers and cut budgets there is no longer even the pretence of education and rehabilitation. These days it is strictly Punishment Only. And not so heavy on Responsibilities when it comes to screws or the care that is supposed to be demanded of prisons. This was shockingly shown up by the racist murder in HMP Feltham. Feltham has been described as terrible by various Prisons Inspectors but nothing changed. Nor at Wormwood Scrubs. One damning report after another was met in the same way. 'Oh that report was three months ago, you should see the changes we've made since then.' In reality we have no chance of seeing anything or, therefore, of challenging this glib irresponsibility. As it is New Labour's solution to damning reports is to undermine and then get rid of the Prison Inspectorate.

If things are so much worse why then publish this memoir now? For one thing opportunity. Some of the stories appeared singly in *Edinburgh Review* and *Passport*, but as a book I have until now been fucked over by a spectrum of 'left wing' publishers. But also because there is an irony to the 'golden age' for there was plenty of punishment then too. Plenty of it, but resistance too and this book is an unsentimental celebration of the class spirit and solidarity of many cons. It is still great when 'resistance gets its own reward,' life would be too hard if not. Fighting the right fights with cunning and solidarity, and winning, that possibility has not been finished off in these repressive times. It is amazing that still now, convict solidarity and resistance still continues in some prisons at some times.

John Barker, September 2006

Bending the Bars

PRISON STORIES

EARLY DAYS: BRIXTON

I HAD NEVER BEEN in prison before. After four days in Albany Street police station Brixton felt quiet, clean, spacious. It was the middle of the afternoon, they had opened Reception especially for the four of us, me, Jim, Chris and Stuart Christie. They had us down as the Angry Brigade along with Hilary and Anna. They would be going through the same business in Holloway. I felt relaxed enough to laugh at 'Reception', a mimicry of the outside world like it really was Her Majesty's Hotel. We were dressed in mimic clothes, they weren't so funny: off-duty uniformed-cop gear, stiff grey trousers and a loud checked jacket. The cops had our own clothes for forensics.

The Reception screw was moderately laid-back. He looked as though he might have been a sailor. He went through some details. I was Buchanan at the time, a flimsy alias, to which he added the number 100484 and a white cell card which was for everyone bar Catholics and Jews. When he'd finished he glanced at my blackening eye.

"Fell over in your cell did you Buchanan?" he said, laughing without menace. It is a fact that many prisoners in British police stations do such a thing, often injuring or killing themselves in the process as if there was something about such places that brought on vertigo or drastic clumsiness.

We were distributed to A Wing which was even more spacious, a museum piece of galleries four floors high. The

Wing SO produced two elderly cons to show us how to fold our bedclothes which would be inspected every day. I was thinking, fucks sake, there really are old lags as I watched. I was given a cell on the ground floor, the Ones. I was locked in with the pillow case stuffed with sheets and prison clothes that I'd been given in Reception. The cell was not at all so spacious but when I lay down on the bed, four days of all-night interrogations, noise, beatings, screams and dirt lost their grip.

I woke up to an outbreak of sounds and tried to work them out, like the sound effects of a radio play. The door crashed open and the sounds were louder. I got up and looked out of the door. There were cons everywhere, on the upper landings both sides of the wing; on the staircases; and on the Ones carrying plastic plates and cups towards a hotplate set up there. Others were talking, exchanging newspapers, smoking cigarettes. I dug a cup and plate out of the pillow case and moved towards the hotplate. This was overseen by screws and manned by cons. There was a continuous flow, plate after plate, a square of potatos laced with shredded meat, bread, a dob of marge, a dob of jam, tea. More technique was needed for dinner with the moulded metal trays which we picked up and were taken back every midday. Without a steady hand soup, gravy and custard would swim over the tray ridges, brown circles forming slow and greasy in the yellow. As it was I got my tea, got looked over and was banged up again.

Some time later the door crashed open again and a screw shouted Slop Out. This time just a few cells were open. Most cons were wearing just vests and enormous underpants. Some carried piss-pots to the toilet area, a three cell space they called the recess. I walked along for the sake of it and had a quick wash. A giant at the next sink asked if I'd just arrived and was one of them bombers.

"Alleged," I said.

He was tickled. "That's the style son, you stick to that," he said. "There's a lot of no-good cunts in here."

The door opened once more about an hour later, a con stood there with a metal bucket shouting, Teas Up. I rushed back to my table, grabbed a mug and held it out. I felt like one myself as he poured it out. A screw two paces behind slammed the door as the con moved on. It was only then I realized why so many cons were down to vests and pants. It was August, it was hot, the cell window was small and high up, the part that opened even smaller. The rough brown uniform I'd got at Reception in exchange for the cop gear itched like fuck.

The bed sheets though were clean and cool, a luxury after the stiff rags of the police station. In the days there I'd felt quite enough misery: rage for having let the cops get a grip of me; catastrophe feelings, seeing enough to know that they could and would stictch up a tight case against me; the sound of screams doing its work in my head, a downward spiral of helpless sympathy, fear and rage. It was all made real by the insufferable confidence and random brutality of the cops in their position of total power. In short, a comprehensive tour of misery.

As I lay in the quiet of the cell the ballast of my body took over. It felt warm and real, it was all in one piece. I hugged my knees up to my chest and was warmed by knowing we'd all held our ground in the police station. Suddenly the light went out. I fell asleep knowing it wasn't the end of the world.

I didn't take in much of the nick in those first few days. The routine was simple enough, banged up 23 hours a day there wasn't time for it to get complicated. We talked between each other on exercise, assessing just how much shit we were in. Jim and I reckoned we were neck high whereas the others looked like straightforward purge victims.

Before our first remand appearance I'd woken up a bit. There'd been a demo for us outside the walls, for the Fire Brigade some witty bastard said. We picked up some of the geography of the place on escorted trips to the Visits area. Brixton looked like a museum-piece that did its job. Then one day I looked seriously at the shape of Jim's prison gear and looked at mine. Humiliation plus, not just itchy but a dirty brown colour.

At the same time I learned what a shit parcel was. The fact is we were banged up continuously from 7pm till 7am, equipped with a murkily transparent plastic pisspot. The unwritten, unspoken official deal was that if you need a shit in the night, the pisspot was the place for it. It did after all have a lid. In reality the pisspot was not up to the job, the cell would stink. One day I asked a con about a work party of prisoners in grey outifts who were combing the ground by the cell-blocks and bucketing up newspaper cylinders. He told me the cons were some of the small number of short-term convicted guys in the jail and what they were collecting. For a shit at night you needed a piece of newspaper, that was the place for it. Then it was parcelled up and dropped out through the small opening in the barred cell window.

"You're having me on, " I said.

"What, winding you up? No, it's the sensible solution if you think about it."

I visualized it, thought about it, and realized it was true. So when I looked at Jim in his clothes I said, "We look like shit-parcels on legs." He looked down mournfully at his shoes that were slipper like sawn-off winklepickers; then at the good showing of leg between sock and trouser bottom, it was amazing how in the same pair of trousers the legs could be so short and the crotch so low; then up to the lapel-less jacket, all in the same shit brown.

"There must have been a designer on this," he said.

"What, a sadist in the Home Office with a free hand?"

"How else can you view the evidence, this goes beyond incompetence."

The same night I looked at myself and the other cons as we were unlocked for slop out. There we were in our equally ludicrous underpants solemnly carrying our pots. We did not look like dangerous men.

In those early days a big blonde con tried to pick me up. Maybe that's an exaggeration, after all we were only out for about an hour a day so it was only ever some ambiguous bullshit. And he was a bullshitter, master criminal nothing. When his singling me out moved on to ways in which he personally could make my life better in this place, I got pissed off. For one thing there were my friends and other cons I wanted to talk to. So that's what I did, because I wanted to and because it was a matter of pride and freedom.

We gained some respect early on for being so tight-lipped about the case, admitting nothing. In this one respect we were not green. The start of our troubles and the charges against Jake who'd been nicked earlier in the same case, rested on the evidence of two cons he'd shared a cell with, a Mr A and a Mr B.

The day of our second Remand appearance began early with breakfast in Reception. We were On Production, the court requiring regular demonstrations of our existence until we'd been committed for trial. We were back in the cop clothes, looking chic after the browns. This business also involved the fiction that we might get bail. We were not going to get bail but the fiction did have aggravating consequences. It meant we had to hand in our kit, knowing all the while it was a dead cert we'd be back and in a different cell at the end of the day.

We were put into sweat-boxes in a black paddy-waggon. The personal sweat box was more evidence of sadistic design, just high enough to stand up to look out of the tiny window but with a moulded-in seat which made the floor space impossibly narrow. When I did peer out for a glimpse of the

Strand crowded with people looking cheerful in the sun, my body was screwed up, my weight in all the wrong places.

The Clerkenwell court building was run by the cops. They took us over for a few hours in their glum basement cells. Our court appearance lasted two minutes. We screwed out a half hour legal meeting with friends and lovers from Holloway. In the longer afternoon there was a longer journey back through the evening rush hour. It included a detour to stop-off at Rochester Row where cons from all the courts of London were sorted out for all the prisons of London. There were already a score of cons in the big holding cell. A small, dapper guy was excited, telling a giant in a good suit his legal moves.

"You know what my brief's come up with, he's fucking mustard the geezer."

"What's that Tone?" the big guy said like he had other stuff on his mind.

"A fucking writ of Mandamus. He's going to slap it on the Regional this week. There'll be some arseholes twitching down there."

The other con sighed, like he thought the Regional wouldn't give a monkey's one way or another.

"The beauty of it is, with a Mandamus the brief says there's got to be a result, dirty bastards."

"Yes Tone," the big guy said.

The final leg through the South London traffic was a killer. I was sticky and knackered but dragged myself up for a last look at the leafy trees of Brixton Hill. We got our tea in a Reception cell with some cheerful young guys out of West London. They'd had a good run with some Post Office books and a stamp, and clued us in about verbals.

"You wait till you get your depositions," one said. "DS Shithead will have given you the works. Half of them should be writing plays."

This didn't sound so good but their cheerfulness was a

tonic. Everything they said suggested theirs was just a temporary setback.

We were processed again, got a new kit and moved on to the large post-Reception cell where there were already fifty-odd cons, the room full of smoke. The talk was about prisons. Someone said how'd they'd freaked out the American Indians more than anything else when the USA state was carving them up. They knew that in battle it might be their last day alive, that was natural, but to be locked up day in day out, it drove them mad. Someone else asked what it would be like if they weren't single-sex institutions. It would make it impossible for them to get their rules and regulations taken seriously, he reckoned. Jim said it was a ludicrously abstract debate. Somehow we got from there to how it was I was down as a translator while the others were unemployed. A young Scots con leaned over.

"This is a true story, I wound up caught bang to rights on a ready-eye in Kensington, gun and all. In the station there's this sergeant, oldish guy, doing my antecedents. What's my occupation. So I tell him the truth, painter and director. You know what he said?"

We all looked up as one.

"He said, Sonny, if you want to play with guns you're a car dealer. And he wrote it down just like that, said I'd get more time on the strength of it."

"He's out of date," another con said, "it's Company Director for big bird these days."

A crash course in certain realities of Life this was, but by nine o'clock I was too tired to take in any more. I stayed like a zombie smoking too many cigarettes till I was called out after eleven. We were formed into a party and escorted down a long corridor and through B wing, the nutters wing. I'd been through it in the day, seen mean-looking screws in white jackets and trayloads of different coloured pharmaceuticals doled out into small plastic cups. At night it was eerie in the half light. Screams and moans, shadow faces at the open grilles in the cell doors, whispers for snout and the sound of sobbing. Back on A Wing I got a cell on the Fours. I fell straight on the bed but couldn't sleep. My head was pounding, what we came to call an adrenalin hangover.

Remand appearances were once a week so this sixteen hour day became regular. I still looked forward to it for the few minutes with Anna and Hilary in the corridor even with the SBs right on top of us. After six days of bang-up it was something different and the adrenalin that went with it was OK till nine. After that it was always the same, wishing more passionately than at any other time that I was somewhere else.

One night we were even longer in Reception. There'd been talk of a con called Jack who'd been down that morning to go on trial some place in Sussex. Jack could see the obvious, what kind of snotty rich bastards he'd get on the jury; knew they'd be the same kind of people whose houses he was supposed to have screwed. He'd refused to go. They'd had to carry him out of the wing. In the court he'd refused to co-operate except to say he demanded to be tried by his peers at the Bailey. And he'd swung it. It was inspiring news, great when resistance gets its own rewards. Inspiring, but I was still knackered come nine o'clock. This time we didn't move off till midnight. There was a full moon and the route was different. Someone said, But we're on A Wing. The screws said nothing. We landed up in F Wing and were allocated cells by a Lebanese fraud merchant who ran the paperwork logistics. I knew about F Wing, that most cells were two'd up but it was still strange to get banged up in a cell where another con was fast asleep. Take nothing for granted was the lesson, not to get fazed when suddenly cut off from the known which in my case had been A Wing.

The crash course in inter-personal skills began with a Manchester con of fifty who'd been in and out for years. On his first stretch in Strangeways his granny had come up on a visit and kept looking at his leg. "She was looking for my ball and chain," he said. Another time he gave me a roll-up from some tobacco I'd never seen before, Black Beauty. It was dry and after a few drags my head was in a spin. I laid down in a hurry and went with it. He laughed. You don't have to buy so much burn with this," he said. Not a problem for me, I was getting plenty of fags off generous visitors.

There being a bed on either side of the cell there wasn't so much floor space so we were slow and careful when we moved. Maybe sensitivity is too big a word but that's how it had to be. We knew we didn't have that much to say to each other but it didn't become a strain. Jim had it worse, banged up with a guy who thought Armley jail, Leeds, was the business. He'd say, Much better food, in Leeds. You wouldn't believe how good the visits are, in Leeds. Then he'd say he didn't mind blacks, as long as long as they were law-abiding. Jim was going mad trying to get across that this was a mite hypocritical.

It was still 23 hours bang-up broken up by exercise and mealtimes. At ten in the morning the tannoy came to life with SEND DOWN YOUR SICK. I had a picture of Lazarus in the bible picking up that bed and walking. In the afternoon an ice-cream van would crank out scraps of Greensleeves. The timetable of sounds grew into days and weeks and the reality of prison, of being locked up in a small space day in and day out got to me. The recuperation period was long gone. I had a nightmare featuring myself as a head in a wheelchair.

I read the newspapers and felt depressed instead of the rage I'd felt on the out. Now there was even less I could do about anything. There were reports of some Leeds cops charged with the death of David Oluwale, a Nigerian living on the road. I'd been active on the case before I was nicked. I read the same brute confidence of the cops that I'd now experienced for myself. The arrogance stayed with them in the court. Their lawyer objected to the victim being called Mister Oluwale. He said his only claim to this title was that he'd been a frequent inmate of Her Majesty's Prisons. Another headline read, OLUWALE WAS A SOCIAL PROBLEM. They'd got the modern patter and the truncheons. The cops got off and about the same time the Compton report came out concerning the treatment of Irish republican prisoners. They put some tricky philosophers on the job who came up with the idea that there were Human and Inhuman ways of being nasty to prisoners. It was decided that in this case it was merely human nastiness and that this was therefore a matter of ill-treatment rather than torture. Since it concerned prisoners I took this filth personally. I held on to the Mangrove trial and its inspiration. They'd defended themselves and got off.

One especially hard week was two'd up with an upper class git who kept telling me that his being there was a mistake. He also complained that the nick was not being run efficiently, that such sloppiness would not have been tolerated in the army. By the end of the week I worked out he'd been doing a cheap and nasty fraud on poor people. The next week though I was ashamed to discover that despite my dislike I must have been trapped in my polite upbringing, he caught hold of me on exercise and told me what a terribly uncouth man he was now two'd up with, and tried to involve me in the drama of his sureties. It was easy to tell the cons who'd got bail but were waiting on sureties to turn up with the money. They were the ones with furrowed brows; the ones who'd whisper confidentially with a twinkle in the eye, Wednesday, it's definite. Come Thursday it was embarrassing to see them on the yard. By the time this fucker started on the same bollox, I was sick of the whole thing: I'd heard I was in line for fifteen years minimum, this guy was going to get two at the most. On top of which I didn't like him. So I told him I didn't give a fucking monkeys about his sureties and felt better for it.

Around this time a yachting pal of Prime Minister Heath got quick bail on a major dope smuggling rap. Meanwhile Home Secretary Maudling made a speech against violence in which he included drug-dealing which he called violence against the human spirit. I thought of those American Indians and having been down to smoking dried banana skin I was dead pleased to get my hands on a bit of Leb.

Christmas came around. A tree appeared on the wing. At least it would not be like every other day. I was banged up with a moody Yugoslav at the time. We got a couple of Number Ten fags as our present off the Governor and a cup of weird coffee. My cell mate got the hump at the hotplate when they rationed his roast spuds and blanked his dinner. We shared mine. On Boxing Day we got taken over to the chapel to see a John Wayne film. The projector lurched into action, stalled, restarted and then broke down again. The screw operating it looked at it. More and more screws came to stand round and look at it. After ten minutes they decided it was terminal. That gave us more pleasure than the film could ever do.

THE SIT-DOWN

WHEN COMMITTALS were over at the end of January we were able to keep the same cells and settled in on the fours. There were three of us on this wing and for the first time were able to exert a minimal control of our own lives. We had a single cell and a two'd up one between us and worked a sort of rota so that we all had time in the single. It involved minor paperwork aggravation for the screws but we'd become better at hustling. We also made some good friends like the two Eddies. One was a beautiful red indian from South London. He'd been grassed up in the worst way, ambushed by the cops on the job itself, a ready-eye. Scots Eddie should have been top of the class in university or playing midfield for one of the Dundee clubs. The screws had him down as a mouthy bastard.

In the meanwhile the boredom of all-day bang up wore on. It was broken by 2 half-hour exercises round and round the yard, and fifteen minute visits. These were the focus for the anger the whole routine created. More than anything else they made it clear we were guilty till proved innocent. They were brief and took place with a wired glass between con and visitor. One guy's son asked him when he'd be finished cleaning the windows.

The glass ran the whole length of the Visits room at waist height. The length was broken into thinly partitioned cubicles. These were open at the back to a passage which screws patrolled. Some times they tried to listen in and were always hustling us to finish before the quarter hour was up. At the bottom of the glass were small grilles on both sides. What a performance. Twisting your head down to listen, up to see your visitor's lips moving. Fifteen minutes in a fish tank.

It got up everyone's nose and it was something the nick could change. It did not need Acts of Parliament or new buildings. The angry feeling built up around the same time the miners were showing that what the State said was impossible was possible if you fought seriously enough. We were entertained by Mr Heath and his cabinet wimping on about the miners not playing the game when they made pickets effective.

Some weeks later in April we heard of one or two sit-downs in other jails. Here was a straightforward way of saying we were seriously pissed off. We could fuck up their routine; show them and ourselves that their power was not absolute, that it depended on our acceptance. Up and down the Fours we talked about it. There were alternating feelings of how strong we were, that a sit-down would be a doddle; how difficult, that we'd never get it together on the whole wing. There was a real factor here, a fast turnover of cons as trials came and went. There was also plenty of bullshit - I'd do it but with all the grasses and gas-meter bandits on the wing it won't work — that kind of thing.

At that time radios were not allowed. When two were smuggled in, an informal rota developed on the Fours for a night's listening. Music sounded fresh but no one took liberties with the volume and they didn't get captured. That made us feel stronger. One day Frank, a big guy who stole jewels, said friends of his on A wing were getting ready for some action. Friends of his would be serious people. They wanted to go first and us to perform the following day. One afternoon we were taken a long route back from visits and caught a glimpse of A wing sat down on the yard.

The next afternoon I was called for a visit. Exercise would have started by the time I'd got back and I'd have no chance of getting on the yard once our sit-down had started. I made out to the screw I had the needle with the visitor and blanked it.

It wasn't a bad afternoon for mid-April. I thought I could feel a definite tension as we went out of the gates on to the yard and that the screws must sense it too, never mind all the oranges in pockets and everyone sweatered-up. Frank had said we'd get some supplies from A wing but we didn't really think about that. I was with Jim and a couple of other mates. There were the usual knots of talk moving around the figure-of-eight path on the yard but this time heads were bobbing up out of the different groups to look around, mine too.

"What are we supposed to be doing, leaving it right till the end?" someone asked.

It was stupid, feeling tense over such a little thing when I had lawyers saying I was going to get twenty, maybe twentyfive years. I couldn't take the numbers on board but this really was a nothing in comparison.

"A few minutes before the end, we don't want people going in before we start," Jim said.

Eddie came over. "I'm ready for a picnic, what's happening?"

Behind me someone said, "There's too many no-good cunts and chancers in this place for anything to go off."

We were still moving around, half in browns, half in our own clothes, all overdoing the normal look.

"Is Frank giving a sign?"

"You can't leave it all down to Frank," I said. "They're always looking for ringleaders, as if the rest of us were sheep."

We must have done twenty laps by then, maybe another fifteen minutes of exercise. Jim started explaining how adrenalin works. There was enough sloshing around in my body, it was difficult to finish a sentence. It must have been that everyone thought it had gone on long enough, walking around. "Lets sit down now," someone said. Forty-odd of us slowed down and bunched up. We came to a stop next to the biggest piece of grass inside the figure-of-eight. A second of hesitation and we sat down. Very quickly there were a hundred or so and I felt free my body, pleasure in the prospect of unlimited time in the open air after months boxed in. As exercise was called to a close about sixty cons went quickly back onto the wing, others carried on walking.

All told there had to be around 200 of us still out.

"That wasn't so difficult was it," Eddie said.

The talk opened up again, we'd broken back into the here and now: we weren't waiting for it to happen, it was happening. The PO issued an order for us to return to the wing. He looked small.

"So much for all that bollox about most people not wanting to know," I said.

"What'll happen next?" someone asked.

A con I didn't know said, "They'll leave it a while so they don't look panicky, then some whiteshirt will come out, ask what it's all about and tell us they'll talk about it if we go back to our cells."

"They'll be ringing the nick with old bill," Frank said. "We'll give them a long cold night."

The cons walking around looked different already. They looked great, no more Brixton shuffle. From A wing there were shouts of support from shadows moving at the barred windows. Frank went to one on the Ones to talk to his mate. I shared an orange with Scots Eddie. Jim was stretched out on the grass taking it all in. Suddenly a large group of screws funneled out of the wing gate. Cons talking to the barred faces in A wing turned to look, we all tensed for a moment. The screws took up positions on the far edges of the yard. Chairs were brought out for them. Only the screws with dogs stayed on their feet. Jim, me and Sadiq decided on a walk. We set a good pace round the figure-of-eight and talked about food, fantasised, constructed immense menus. A Cypriot guy joined us and got in the mood, described a weekend off in his country in exquisite detail.

How they'd go off into the mountains with a bag of grass and a flagon of wine. They'd find a sheep up there, kill it and make kebabs over an open fire. With the sun in my face there were tastes in my mouth, smells in my nose. I was weak at the knees.

The cons stood by A wing windows were coming away with chocolate bars, fruit, cups of tea. The big plastic mugs had been gotten out of an office window. Faceless cons behind the bars were pouring into them. I'd been spoiled, only kebabs and wine would do, but was impressed by A wing efficiency. Next time round Frank said they'd send out blankets come the dark, they'd already been through it and knew the score. He suggested we get everyone together to sort out our demands. We passed on the message and in a short time were nearly all together on the piece of grass where we'd sat down in the first place. We all stood up in a rough circle so the screws couldn't see who was talking. A con called Richie told me and Jim we should be careful as there would be some screws' men amongst us. I said if we started worrying about that we'd never get anything done. The sit-down could not have been such a surprise, A wing had done it already and no doubt there were grasses on the wing but so what.

"We've got to ask for all the visits to be open, they've got them in convicted jails," someone said.

"That'll take time, they'll have to change the whole Visits area."

"That's their fucking problem," Frank said. "They're getting paid plenty. All they've got to do is take out the glass."

"We must concentrate on the fact that we are innocent," Sadiq said.

"Speak for yourself."

"We are all innocent," went up the cry, some faces serious and plenty of wry smiles.

"As innocent as the day I was born," Scots Eddie said in an assumed Edinburgh voice.

Jim said out loud, "Why don't we ask for all visits to be open with no cutback on the number of visits. Set a time limit for the conversion and have one open visit per week in the meanwhile. They could do it in the other room that the convicted guys have."

"What about more association, we're getting fuck all, they get plenty in the convicted jails."

"What about the food."

"Food?" The Cypriot's scorn was cosmic, "what food."

"They spend more on food for the dogs."

"I've seen the sacks for the porridge, third grade it says."

"It's pigmeal."

The meeting was breaking up into many meetings. After months the lid was coming off. A couple of screws had come closer to try and hear who was saying what. Frank had a quiet voice and had to shout.

"All these demands are fair enough but we've got to concentrate on the Visits first, that's what A wing did."

There was general agreement despite more talk of food and association. The cry went up WE WANT OPEN VISITS NOW.

We were just about to start walking again when a PO came over.

"You've made your point lads. If you go back to your cells now everything will be all right and we'll look into your grievances. Otherwise I don't know."

I hate being called Lads and started snarling. The con who'd predicted the PO's line of chat said, "Look governor, we're unconvicted and at the best we're getting one open visit a month, it's not on."

"You won't get anywhere by refusing lawful orders like this and I have already issued you with one to return to your cells. We'll see about a delegation to the Governor in the morning."

Given A wing's performance, this was wishful thinking.

"Who do you think you're kidding," some said.

"We'll come in when we feel like it."

The PO shook his head and walked off.

The sky was darkening with some last grey-pink dashes. A pile of greatcoats were brought out for the seated screws. Jim, me and the two Eddies were walking again, talking about crime. I was saying that in my very limited experience it was self-perpetuating because the money was spent like water. "It seems so easily come by it feels like toy money."

"You obviously have an innate sense of the labour theory of value," Jim said.

"You what," Eddie said.

"That your labour time is the only real measure of value."

"Sounds like the kirk to me," Scots Eddie said. "Work hard and save, I've had enough of that to last me a lifetime."

"So how do you spend your ill-gotten gains?"

"Quickly."

"Exactly, so then you've got to do another stunt. The odds against getting captured have got to shorten."

"No, I've just got to use my brains more."

Suddenly the whole yard was lit up like it was Highbury for a night game. The jail floodlights had come on and cued in the rain. It fell as sparkling needles in the lights. The screws rushed into their greatcoats. Blankets began to appear through the bars of A wing where some cons had moved for a bit of shelter. Me, I was revelling in it, hadn't felt the rain or been out at night for eight months but a trickle of cons went back to the wing and gave themselves up. Jim said a few had gone in earlier. I hadn't noticed and no one cared too much. There was a volley of abuse aimed at the the screws' quarters which overlooked the wall nearest the yard, some fifty yards away.

"Does he have you slopping out at night missus."

"Does he bang you up when he goes out"

Then a snatch of song, WHY DO YOU LIVE WITH FUCKING FILTH, WHY DO YOU LIVE WITH FILTH

"Does he put the kids on bread and water?"

The rain was beating down harder, the grass chewed up. Two tall cons with long hair and beards were wearing blankets like ponchos and had rolled their brown trousers up to their knees. I was entranced, so stylish, they might have been strolling across Hampstead Heath or the Rif mountains.

The same PO came out again and we gathered slowly from all corners of the yard. "The Deputy Governor will see three spokesmen if you go back to your cells," he said.

"What guarantees?"

"No spokesmen," we shouted, "he sees all of us or none."

He retreated again, said we were being unreasonable. But soon after a body of cons made their way back to the wing, we could see them being forced to go in one at a time. There was no abuse from the yard except for guys who'd gone in with blankets. I was wishing I had one, the novelty of the rain was wearing off."

"How many left?" I asked.

"A bit over half, a hundred and twenty maybe," Jim said.

We decided that a definite time limit might be an idea, otherwise there might be a steady drift back and we'd end up looking weak. Everyone with blankets had made them into ponchos. The screws looked like they were getting more miserable and uptight by the moment. Fucking great, that cheered me up no end. But on the next lap, however many hundreds it was, we put our point to Frank. He agreed, it was obvious we were losing people at a steady rate. Someone else said it would be a cop-out.

"Maybe but we want to go in strong, not straggling back," Frank said.

"We could demand a hot meal when we get back in, that way it would be on our own terms," I said, feeling how empty my stomach. Someone else said yes, and that we'd broken the ice; we'd done it once, we could do it again.

By this time it had become a meeting. Jim said, "We're reckoning we should set a definite time limit, midnight say, later if you like, but a definite time so we don't get any more wandering in. Also demand a hot meal for when we do go back."

"You are a moderate," Sadiq said.

I had heard Jim called many things but never that. For a moment it looked like he had the hump. Then he said, "I'll have you as a character witness at my trial." The two of us fell about laughing.

"Why midnight, we might as well stay now, we can't get much wetter," someone said.

"Yes, lets just stay, no time limits."

"I bet you'll find more going in."

"No, everyone who's still here, we're over the worst."

We did though decide to meet up again in an hour.

The yard had become a surreal stadium with the lights, rain and field turned to mud. Me, Jim, the two Eddies and our new-found Cypriot pal found a half-sheltered spot by the ribbed brickwork where the A wing recesses were. The wing's cell lights went out. I remembered my very first night, one minute the light was on, next it was off. Since we'd been on the Fours we'd got into bargaining with the night screw for another hour or two. Some obliged, some did not but you could never tell which screws, at most you could see an eye the other side of the spyhole.

We brightened up when a black con started doing a top notch gymnastics work-out on the grassy mud. Cartwheels, big, big somersaults, and handstands. We cheered like crazy. Jim and I broke into Singing in the rain/Just singing in the rain/What a glorious feeling/We're hap hap happy again. This accompanied by heavy-footed tap-dancing. Even the paths were muddy now. Our feet made only squelchy sounds. Tap dancing needed crisp ones, we tried clicking sounds.

The gymnastics ended with your man slipping on a cartwheel. He lay on the muddy ground laughing. Wild cheering. The screws were disappearing into themselves, heads on chest, rain running off their cap peaks. We were cheering. A new song started and was taken up all round the yard.

Go Home You Screws/Go Home You Bums

Go Home You Screws/Go Home

Go Home You Bums/Go Home You Screws

Go Home You Bums/Go Home

That was the gist of it, sung to the tune of Auld Lang Syne.

Bums and screws came at different times from different parts of the yard. Cons still walked in groups but sang the tune as one. At the end a voice shouted, That's if you've got homes to go to you scumbags.

The stadium feeling had its own momentum. Another chant started immediately.

YOU NEED US, WE DON'T NEED YOU, our arms shooting up on the US.

In this mood it was a shock to see a few cons go back in and one of them, the fucker, he'd been mouthing off about staying out all night not an hour earlier. Most everyone saw it, most everyone was feeling the cold and wet. So we met up again, drifting to that patch where we'd first sat down. this time there was general agreement we should say Twelve o'clock. Only one voice said, I told you so. We called over to the PO and felt good when he fairly scurried over. We told him what we wanted, a meal guaranteed. He said he couldn't guarantee it and anyway, it would take a lot of organising at this time of night.

Many voices said more or less the same, that he'd better go and organise it, what was he being paid for. He said the Governor and the prison officers had been very tolerant and that we should go in now. Many voices spoke, the gist was, don't give us that bollox, go and sort it out.

He went off.

More chanting began, some cons thought the press would be outside. WE ARE HUMAN BEINGS.

"The most emotive words in the vocabulary," Jim said, "when put together. For all those hypocrites in the United Nations, when they say human beings it's unanswerable."

"If it's people in other countries," I said.

We got back to our place by the wall. I took deep, deep breaths. The night air was clearing months of stuffy cells and standardcell pipe heat out of my head. The trampled grass gave off its special night time smell. The colours were wild: the muddy green with its own light gold sheen from the lights which lit only the stage of path and grass, leaving the screws as spectators in the dark; the walking cream blankets; the dull yellow of the Wing bricks. The feeling that it was a stadium must have been common, someone started up with YOU'LL NEVER WALK ALONE. It was taken up all round the yard. I didn't know all the words, just the chorus, made noises for the rest that were swallowed into one crescendo after another. There were solo voices from A wing. We raised out arms in acclaim. A shadow from behind the bars disappeared then a hand came out from the broken leaded panes. Something dropped from between the bars. A bar of chocolate, Bourneville, my favourite. What timing. I picked it up from the ground, rustled the wrapping and broke it five ways.

What taste, slowly melting in the mouth, warm chocolate soaking into every taste bud and pore. Magic, we shouted to the dim face in the darkened cell.

On the other side of the yard, the PO appeared again. We didn't fancy leaving our bit of half-shelter but saw an arm beckoning from under a poncho. That got us moving.

"It's a deal," the con said. "We go in at midnight which is about twenty minutes, and we get a meal."

Now that we'd won the demand Jim, me and Scots Eddie began to feel some doubts. If we'd won this easily maybe we could have won more. We reassured ourselves.

"The important thing is we're going in together and on our own terms."

"We've broken the ice. They know that and we know it, there won't be all that poncing about convincing people next time."

I figured they'd be very short-sighted to fuck us over on the visits and wondered how far we could push in other areas before they showed their claws.

There were around a hundred of us left, we kept close and launched into QUE SERA, SERA / WHATEVER WILL BE, WILL BE

As soon as it seemed like flagging someone would give it new heart. It went on and on, faster and faster till no one could keep up. Windows in the screws' quarters opened up.

"Don't let him take it out on you," someone shouted.

WE ARE THE CHAMPIONS

Then another chorus of YOU'LL NEVER WALK ALONE.

It tailed off ragged.

"Think of a chant," someone said. I chanced my arm, CONS FIVE-SCREWS NIL, I shouted. Nothing worse than starting a chant no one takes up. I kept it going a few times hoping some bugger would take it up. No deafening roar came but enough of a shout to save me from mugging myself off. It flurried and wore out just as the screws moved in towards us. It looked like the PO who'd done all the talking was in charge of the reception posse by the wing gates. We moved in as a crowd till there was a thin string at the end, me at the back feeling suddenly isolated. We were being let in one at a time, a re-assertion of screw power. From the back I could see ten guys in front being herded through a narrow corridor of blue raincoats. I felt a hard nudge in the back and for the first time saw the hatred on the screws' faces. The fag was knocked out of my hand, the corridor was a corral. I fixed a set smile, told myself how pathetic they were. A thin wiry screw we called Wandsworth tried to trip me up as I went through the gates. I rode it as they called me a cunt and a long-haired cunt.

In the wing, cons were being directed to their own cells. It felt like divide and rule in practice and I had a single cell. I saw Jim on the stairs. We shrugged and saw urns arriving at a table set up on the ones. That was reassuring. One part of me knew they'd be stupid to renege on the deal or start handing out stick because I felt confident there would be a heavy comeback from our side, but I hated being dependent on them keeping their word. There was always the power of resentment and their instinct to slap down trouble.

There were plenty of screws on each landing. One followed me down the Fours and I was banged up. I sat down in the hard-backed chair and faced the door. Adrenalin swilled about. Outside SOs and screws were shouting out the numbers they were accountable for. They'd made a cock-up on the Fours and I could hear footsteps coming down the landing, spyholes lifted and dropped. Five, Four, Three, Two, mine. I relaxed as the footsteps passed on. Through the window I heard someone shout that we were being let out one at a time.

By the time my door opened I'd got wired up again, thinking the bastards were going to leave me out. Nothing I could have done about it and I was starving. At last I was unlocked and went down for the food with Del. There were screws all over the place. In Brixton it was the practice for cons to serve out the food. It was great to see the screws having to do it. On the hotplate the screws were acting like it wasn't really them at all, except they were sullen with it. Down came a razor-thin slice of corned beef, down came some beans. I picked up as much bread as possible. The screw at the end tried to flick a dob of marge into the beans but I was too quick.

As a tea it didn't rate as much more than a symbol, next time we should negotiate the fucking menu. The wing seemed bigger than ever, St Pancras station with lino and an army of occupation. Back in the cell hunger and a sense of victory beat the adrenalin hands down. I laid waste to a mountain of bread.

A FEW WEEKS LATER our trial began and we were back on A wing. Only at weekends did we catch up with what was going down. There had been another sit-down but we'd missed it, being at the Bailey. Instead, back in the cell after a day of trial it was good to return the compliment and throw chocolate bars down on to the yard.

One Sunday it was really fine weather, a real joy to be on exercise. Lying down on the grass Jim was asking if this fucker on the wing really had gone QE.

I hadn't felt the sun so hot for months. From what seemed like far away I heard a voice say, "Yes, kept it quiet for months and I'd thought he was really sound."

"Me too, I never sussed him."

"From what I've heard he did a deal with the DS months ago and strung along the rest of the firm, Colin and them for months. Diabolical. And they've smelled nothing when they're living on top of each other on the wing. Months of it."

"I can see the day we'll all have to go to work on our own, you know what I mean. They were all pals for years but he's still lollied them up."

"Doesn't do much for trust does it," I said.

I stayed horizontal, feeling the sun stroking me under the skin and must have dozed off because the next thing I heard was the PO calling the end of exercise. I looked up and saw the wing gates had been opened. I really did not want to go in out of the sun. A screw moved to the gate with a board in his hand ready to tick us off.

"Too nice to go in," someone said.

Oh yes.

"It's not often we get weather like this, a long exercise is called for."

I made a pillow of my shirt and vest. Jim started to tell me how good the sun was for a body. He mentioned an essential D vitamin.

"I thought it was C vitamins, that's what it says on Cornflakes."

"Cornflakes," he said with a sneer, "Cornflakes. I don't know why I bother explaining things to you. It's a D vitamin. Without it, lassitude."

I said I could feel it was doing me good, I didn't need to be told why. He called me a fucking hippy. By then the screws were already into their routine, their chairs out on the yard.

Round about six thirty it started to cool. We knew we'd want to be going in soon. A con called Charlie said, "I suppose we'd better make a demand or two to keep them happy."

"How about the food."

"That'll do. If it was just because we like sunbathing they'd throw a wobbler."

It was true. For this afternoon we had improved our standard of living, not asked for it to be improved. A great day off from the Bailey. My face was stretched and tingly from the sun.

WEIGHED-OFF

THE VAN was the same we'd had for months. Its black windows made the wet streets filmy under the sodium lights. They looked that much colder. The difference was that now there were just the two of us and we'd been weighed off. There were times when the six months trial had seemed endless, then suddenly everything was on the hurry-up. After all the ritual and sleepy afternoons the court set-up got moving when they finally got to the point of the business, verdicts, sentences. The jury had made a faltering, courageous plea for clemency. There was a loving farewell to the four acquitted, a scraping of chairs to let them out of the dock. Downstairs a few words about mitigation. Mitigation? What could be said, Sorry and that but this has gone on for long enough, a joke's a joke but I think I'll go home now.

The cops were uptight they hadn't got more bodies going down, but after the jury had been out for three days they were relieved to be getting convictions at all. If not traffic duties and purple rage for the cops, five quid fine cases for the Prosecution. As it was we were weighed off in the dusk. The sentence was mounting up, Fives, Eights, Tens but at the end the magic word, Concurrent. So it was a ten-stretch, five off down to the jury's plea the judge said. Part of me felt relieved, before the trial there'd been lawyers talking of Twenties and Twentyfives. We'd got rid of most of those lawyers.

Cuffed up in the van I tried to make a head-film of the lights shining and breaking up on wet streets. We chain-smoked, the Reception screws would have whatever was left. Ten as a figure didn't sound bad at all but now it was definite that I wasn't going to be legally free for a long time. In my case the cops had framed a guilty man and there'd been so many holes in the frame there'd been half a hope. One boost was that they'd just changed the rules to apply remission to time done on remand. It was retrospective and would be worth a few months.

Into these thoughts the SO spoke into the van. He was a fifty year old pipe smoker who'd been in charge of the escort right through the trial, a specialist in escorts on heavy Bailey trials. We'd never had a serious row with him except when he went on about the abuse aimed at the screws quarters during the summer's sit-downs. Now he said that he'd had a bet on the outcome. He'd been spot-on with the verdicts, four down and four away, but had fancied us for fifteen years apiece. So our maverick jury had done us a favour, and had the SO over.

It was private in the van. A small official operation, a transfer of two bodies from the court to the nick. The blackened windows were designed so that we could see out and no once could see in. The van had always been a break from the packed court, cries from the gallery, its very familiarity. This was the last time, it would all be different. Thoughts went round and round in the tiredness. What would a long-term nick be like, more cushy, crazier? I'd got some picture from experienced cons in Brixton but I didn't know. A picture of the woman I loved in tears as we were lead to our respective vans returned, and with it a cold misery. I forced myself to look out the window and saw signs to WILLESDEN and HARLESDEN. My childhood, its streets and parks that's where I'd spent them and I'd never imagined this in those days. Not in the plot, I'd barely known the existence of prisons. The signposts also said they hadn't pulled a flanker and sent us to Wandsworth, it was the Scrubs, allocation jail for first-timers. The escort cop car ahead suddenly turned off the road. I caught a picture of big gates opening and saw we were expected, bright lights everywhere, walkie-talkies, alsations. My wide-awake, weak-coloured tiredness was heavy on the eyelids.

In a little room off the main Reception area I lost my fags and civilian clothes. I regained my name after months as Buchanan. They went slowly through my pockets before the Brixton screws left with a receipt for goods delivered. The screw behind the table was huge, slow and talked heavy. We stood there, a right pair of dummies, cold too with just a towel round us while the screw took his time over the paperwork. After a while we were waved off to the bath cubicles. A con in blue overalls indicated one for me. The bath had five inches of water. It was lukewarm. I was in and out. Months later on the long-term wing I knew him to be a tosser like a lot of Reception cons, working long hours with screws.

There were exceptions. Another con came back with some greys and the familiar blue-and-white striped shirt.

"I heard about it on the radio, sorry about it, you should have got a medal instead. I put some roll-ups in the pocket."

"Thanks man." One act of support and I felt so much

stronger and the greys he'd given me, they were a good fit. "I appreciate it."

The con smiled. He had long hair, no Wandsworth crop here.

"No worries," he said. I've done most of mine now but I know what it's like to start one. I followed the trial. As it happens I thought you might get a chuck."

In the stores another couple of cons were sat around. They were in no hurry putting together a set of sheets, pants and another set of greys. They wore sneakers, I got the official winklepicker slippers. I tried on the other greys. They'd mugged me off, the trousers were balloons. I felt strong enough to give them a pull. They looked at me, cons looked at me, like I was a troublemaker, but my long-haired mate had given me the confidence to hold out for what I wanted. They got me another pair that fit and then stuffed everything into the pillow case. The last item was a tie. I never got to wear it.

I found Jim back in the Reception area. For tea we were given a grisly pie. It was grey, guaranteed to be returned unmarked by the dozen cons there. We'd all just been weighed off. I drank the grey-brown tea because my mouth was that dry from all the cigarettes. The guy next to me said he'd just got 18 months, it was diabolical, he said. He thought we were cool about everything but then we knew the score a bit from Brixton; we'd got some time under our belts there; we were relieved about it being a ten; and anyway the ten was abstract, it was unreal. I'd seen my mum for a few minutes after sentence was passed and felt ludicrously strong. Counting what I'd done already and assuming I didn't lose too much remission there was only five years and a few months to do. I'd thought it, only.

If this was anything like Brixton we were in for a long wait, I wanted only to be in my bed with the door shut. Instead I tried to get a grasp of five years plus. It was December 1972 so that would take me back to the summer of 1967. It didn't seem that long ago. Then I remembered what a great summer it had been, endless warm nights and cognac. It seemed a long time ago, my first real time abroad. I was very different to how I'd been. So.

I was called out for the Doctor.

"Are you all right?"

"Yes."

"Ever had any serious illness?"

"No."

"All right then, next."

This laconic back-and-forth lasted long enough for me to see my file with CATEGORY A stamped all over it. Jim's file had been the same. We knew from a spell of it in Brixton that it would make things that bit tighter, but perversely it made us feel more important. It was a Danger To The State certificate. I wished only that I was a danger to the state. More importantly it guaranteed a single cell, a major bonus. We assumed it had been stamped up in the Home Office before the verdicts. The Home Office, how's that for a laugh. Anywhere else it's the Ministry of Internal Security. Only the English could be so brazen, the name suggesting warm fires, slippers and general cosiness while in fact they're smashing down doors and ripping homes apart.

The guy with the eighteen months was getting on my tits. He told me for the third time just how hard he'd been done by. Things being what they were it looked to me like he'd had a result, but then he'd been on bail which can make for some easy fantasies and means you're starting your bird from scratch. All true and so what, the fucker only had a year to do. I told him I'd had enough, I had my own problems.

Around ten I got called out again, they'd forgotten to weigh me. Eleven stone. I'd lost nearly a stone during the trial. It would have been all that staggering about from van to cell with half a hundredweight of depositions in my uncuffed arm four times a day. That and the daily jousting with our polite bastard of a judge. No pig me was how he presented himself to the jury. The fucker had even sent me cough sweets one time I had the flu. It was only once or twice, when it really mattered, that he'd shown his claws.

I remembered long night time waits in Brixton when we'd talked till we dropped, the Women's Movement for one, whether being spontaneously non-sexist was a bogus notion; conscious effort seemed somehow second best but necessary. We talked of everything, fraud techniques, the miners strike, football, verbals, whatever came up. Now I didn't have the energy. A screw came to take my dabs. What, had they changed since Albany Street, had they changed since Brixton? Fingers, thumb; thumb again, palm.

"Just relax the hand," he said.

Relax? It felt like my skin was just waiting to get stuck on the bronze pad and ripped off.

It was some time after midnight we set off for the wing, two-abreast. The rain had left the air clear and a full moon lit up the sky with the overhead searchlights in support. Small clouds raced across the sky. We went down a passage under an awning supported by pillars that ran along a patch of grass. We passed two looming wings before arriving at the last of the four that made up the Scrubs. Inside it was huge, bigger than Brixton. We got our cells stamped CAT A. I made my bed wondering how I could accept years of this without head banging the walls. Instead I lay down and fell asleep.

I woke up to the usual noise of hundreds of guys, got dressed and joined the rush on the landing. After the single cells of Brixton's A wing to which we'd returned for the trial period, this one where some cons were three'd up, was like a behaviourist experiment. It could be rats, ants or cons, only the scale was different. I remembered that the founder of the

English prison system, one Jeremy Bentham, had his brain preserved and exhibited in some public place. There seemed to be a grisly connection, a geography of grey, rotting cells.

It wasn't till Slop Out after breakfast that I saw anyone I knew, a South African accountant fraudster. He asked how he could join the Communist Party or the International Socialists, he didn't care which. When he'd finished his sentence he was due for a deport to South Africa and plenty more bird. He figured he could fight it as a political prisoner if he joined up. It sounded neat but a very long shot.

The exercise yard was still more dour than Brixton's, no grass at all. It was a medium-sized school playground without play. I met someone else I knew slightly who said I could meet friends on other wings at church on Sunday. I saw how high the perimeter walls and that there was an equally high inner fence topped with barbed wire. Brixton was evidently underdeveloped. On the way back someone gave me a newspaper. We were on the front page with a double-page spread inside. Was it really me they were talking about? Were people really reading this bullshit on London streets? It was grotesque, that I was in this same London and had already heard a tube train close by.

A couple of weeks later we were temporarily taken off the A book only to be put back on it for good. Still Jim and me did manage to get two'd up for a fortnight. The first Sunday of this time we went to church. A guy sat down next to us and introduced himself as a pal of Jake's. All round was a hum of talking. The vicar, a thin-faced, bearded rat went through the motions. They even had a choir with all the proper red and white gear on. I recognised the one carrying the cross, a well-spoken psycho who'd got more kicks than money out of a string of tie-ups. The screws sat down either wall. The noise of the talk got louder and the vicar's rage went purple. He exploded, ranting and raving, this was the house of god. The guy next to me slipped me a bit of hash. I'd already been nicked for possession in Brixton and the handover hadn't been that cool. I looked around.

"You're not paranoid are you," the guy said.

"No," I lied.

"It's cool. Anyway are you OK over there, C/A wing's a shithole but you won't be there long."

In the afternoon there was supposed to be another church event, a Salvation Army band. Amazing what we'd do to get out of the cell, hoping one of the Eddie's might turn up. Our cell door was unlocked without the sound of general unlock. I had my hand under the pillow, ready to swallow the hash. There were four screws stood in the door.

"Cell search."

The dope wasn't there. I came out of the cell slowly carrying my sheets and blankets out onto the landing, the regular procedure. I scraped my foot along the floor. Nothing. Well that was it, we were nicked.

I'd only noticed one search on this wing, a twenty minute job. The cells were bare and even radios weren't allowed at this time. The screw on the landing searched the sheets. Nothing there. After fifteen minutes the rest of the wing was unlocked for church. They assembled on the Ones. I thought only that I was fucked, they had to find it. Second time around it was going to be a remission job, maybe an outside court. Terrorist is dope-fiend, that kind of thing.

After an hour they were still at it. It was fucking ridiculous. And another hour during which fearing-the-worst and resignation turned to boredom. The church-party had returned and they were still at it. It would be tea time any minute. I started to feel good, it couldn't go on much longer, they must have missed it. Then a fresh bout of paranoia, maybe they'd found it right off and this was all a wind-up. Finally the screws came out, hot and dusty. Our faces were impassive for want of being anything else.

"Right back in your cell," the lead screw said.

One final flash of paranoia, maybe now he'd produce it. No, they aren't that subtle.

"Keep your cell tidier, it's a pit" the screw said.

What? After two hours, keep your cell tidy. But I wasn't chancing any wisecracks. Oh no. Back in the cell we held it on for a couple of minutes, maybe they would come back. Then the dam burst and we laughed like crazy.

"Yes, well where the fuck is it," Jim said when we banged up again with our Sunday tea. I was down on my hands and knees scrabbling about. We could see they'd had the back of the mirror, that they'd dismantled the bed frame. Two fucking hours of it. I wasn't getting anywhere either. I got excited but it was only a grey breadcrumb.

"Are you sure you didn't lose it coming back from the church?"

No, it was in my hand, dust-coated.

"Too fucking much."

"The perfect place," I said blandly. "They look for all the tricky places but can't see it under their feet."

"Couldn't see it for dust. Keep your cell tidy, " Jim said. He was heaving with laughter.

"It's a neat idea leaving it right out in the open. Mind you, I wouldn't like to bet my future on it."

After tea we rolled up. It tasted good. It felt good, good enough for him to give a discourse on sub-atomic particles and me to make a sustained effort to visualise their form and motion. It was hard, where did one begin and another end? Only next day did we think how it had to have been a set-up and how green we would have been. The guy had only said he knew Jake.

D Wing Wormwood Scrubs

IT HAD BEEN twentythree hour a day bang-up in C/A Wing. It was more or less the same in C Wing, a crazy, head-banging limbo. In my case, on the way to a Dispersal prison, the official terminology for a long-term high-security nick. There was the odd outing to work whenever they had enough screws to take the few of us on Category A the one hundred yards to the workshop. It was a shop making wigwams. They were a real bummer, plastic seams and fuck-knows how many cloth panels to be sewn together on a machine. The screw-instructor was patient but relieved my appearances were so rare.

The Scrubs was special in being a reception prison with its own long-term wing, D wing. I'd been told that's where I was going. I had some mates over there from Brixton, Eddie. Scots Eddie and Sadiq. I saw them now and then in their tailor-made cotton blue strides over in the Visits waiting room. I'd given up on seeing them in the church, the vicar, purple vein pulsating with irritation in his forehead, was getting on my wick, never mind the unctuous mumbo-jumbo.

I'd also heard about D wing long before. It was on a visit to Holloway in preparation for our grotesque appeal. One of the escort screws, a neat, hard-faced family man had said to the laid-back PO in charge that what they needed in D wing was some trouble so they could screw it right down.

It's a con's wing now," he said. The PO was non-committal, he was asking me If It Had Been Worth It.

Jim was shipped out to Wakefield as soon as the Appeal was over. Some times I thought about what the screw had said. I had a long time to think about it, the weeks in C Wing went on and on. The fascist coup took place in Chile. I felt impotent several times only. I remembered sitting with a friend in The Apollo pub just after Allende had been voted into power. We'd predicted such a coup at the time. It was obvious from the start he'd do anything rather than arm the people and that he was therefore sure to get fucked over. But the coup still hurt. I resolved not to be surprised at what was not surprising, yet still angry at what was brutal and outrageous. The *Daily Express* headlined the event by saying that Allende had worn a wig.

When I did eventually get moved it was inconvenient. I had a stake in a long-shot tunnel but what could I do? Having hustled many times for the move it would be a bit sus if I now blanked it. It happened on a Friday afternoon. I packed up the few personal bits and pieces in the cell and took them the fifty-odd yards to D Wing past a building called the Rec where we saw a film once a week. I was allocated a cell on the Twos and two friends dropped by, the Eddies from Brixton. They'd been staunch there and were cheerful here, pleased to see me. They'd been weighed off before me for different things and both wound up with five stretches. They explained that Friday was the one day of early bang-up in the week; that as an A man I could either eat in my cell banged up over dinner and tea-time or eat out on one of the tables on the Ones but not the Rec where some cons ate and had association. They themselves were eating in, they liked to have a bit of privacy in the day. They also told me they had some acid for the Saturday.

By then it was autumn, moving into winter, but that first Saturday the sun was shining bright and warm. I felt free, no need to hurry, from morning unlock we were free till midday dinner and if I'd been Eating Out it would have been right through till 8.30 in the evening. Out on the yard Scots Eddie was in a football game. It was an asphalt yard with goalposts. London Eddie introduced me to a guy I remembered from Brixton, Peter. He'd been staunch on the sit-downs but I'd never really known him. I remembered why. He'd been nicked with his brother-in-law after a string of Post Offices got rifled. They were always together but I hadn't liked the brother-in-law, a flash and mouthy bastard he seemed. That's what I said and Peter didn't get the hump, said yes, he did come across like that but was really sound and was now in Chelmsford. We were walking round the pitch, stopping now and then to look at the game and shout like spectators at a park game. Scots Eddie was a great player, quick on the ball and playing first time passes into spaces the other team hadn't seen. Then we'd move on again and Peter pointed out two of the train robbers, heroes of my childhood in the flesh. They were once-famous guys who'd disappeared for years, who were never heard of except maybe in the odd Colour Supplement as having set the tone for the sixties. They were big guys and looked well. It was re-assuring, they'd already done nearly ten years.

Peter was also talking about music, he had a guitar he said. He was excited when I told him I had a flute and harmonica on the out and told me to get them in as fast as possible. I'd never thought such a thing was possible. Peter was surprised at my surprise. For me, what a pleasure to be able to play again after a two year lay-off. And there were acid trips all round that afternoon.

It came on that afternoon in the sun. I'd taken a couple of trips in Brixton but felt nervous this time, opening up on an uncharted voyage in a place that was free by prison standards. So I sucked the tab nice and slow even though I knew it wouldn't make any difference. It didn't, it came on fast. Sadiq was talking to me. He was a guy I liked but as I felt my whole body rushing and thrilling I no longer wanted to hear his reform plan for Pakistan: how President Bhutto was not listening to his reform plan for Pakistan: how this had resulted in him being framed with some kilos of very good black hash: how bad a thing was this same black both socially, spritually and morally. Sadiq's plan sounded like some utopian capitalism but all I could see was my friends spreadeagled on the small lawn which made up the other half of the exercise area: all I could feel was a glorious rush from toes to head. Some music sounded from a radio. My head was slipping and sliding in technicolour. I started to edge away from Sadiq. I was saying in a voice that sounded far away that we should talk about it some other time.

He gave me a funny look but I couldn't be bothering with that. I joined my friends and laid down on the grass. It was pulsating with the music. When I looked up I saw a tall, elegant-looking con with a golf club. He was playing chip shots with real golf balls against the side wall of the wing. I heard myself say, What the Fuck.

"What?" Eddie said with a smile.

"There's a geezer over there who seems to be playing golf."

"Sure, it's Brian."

My head took off to spacious green clifftops. I could hear seagulls, see little white balls in long arcs dropping in slow, slow motion into crescent-shaped sand pits. A gentle thud. A sparkling slow shower of sand.

"Of course he doesn't have his clubs in his cell," Eddie said practically, "gets them out of the control box on weekend afternoons." I started to laugh, it was rumbling and tumbling out of my stomach. Another picture formed, this gentleman bandit getting nicked on a Spanish golf course next time round. "Surely there must be some mistake", I heard. "If you would just come this way senor I'm sure everything can be resolved." The temptation to wishful thinking on his part, a hope that the British consul would not try and help. I fell back on the grass and closed my eyes. It was some time later I heard Scots Eddie suggest we go to someone's cell where there was a record-player and a smoke. I didn't know the guy with the cell but it didn't matter. We were all quickly horizontal. Hawkwind were playing. Our bodies moved little but became a symphony of dance from inside out. One part of my brain wondered what a passing screw might make of such a sight and realised I had no idea of the time and that at some time we'd have to make a move to get banged up for tea. Then the music caught up every bit of body and brain again and I felt a complete trust in the friends around me. Entirely justified. Some time after they brought me slowly out of the music for the reality of tea. We looked at each other, our faces happy and intense. We laughed and got ourselves together. Out on the landing everything was speeded-up. Cons moved about with purpose. I walked to my cell, the landing rushing towards me like a moving trampoline.

I was amongst the stragglers going through for tea which was served in a room on the Ones made up of two or three cells knocked together with an entrance door at one end, exit at the other. Hot-plates formed a long counter behind which were screws and cons. Another screw stood at the end ticking off names. This was why I had to put in a show. It felt like being in a shuffling ID parade. I told myself to be normal. I did not feel normal, my arm. hand and plate shot out rigid for each item on the menu. I didn't know a single person there, wondered what I was doing there on a Saturday afternoon. Shit. Only, terrific, these people were far weirder than me, it was fucking obvious. Boom. Terrific. I was nearly out of the exit when I heard a voice from a long, long way away. No question, it was directed at me. What, did the buggers expect me to talk as well. My head followed the sound waves to a con behind the hotplate, he seemed to be the source, he was looking at me. Right, my gastric diet and the milk ration, him, the cheeky little fucker who'd not come across with it this morning, said it was not on his list. There seemed a log gap between me speaking and hearing my words. My mouth was dry.

"Well where's my milk then?"

Maybe I looked crazy, either way I could see this lackey going defensive. He was mumbling, something to the effect that he'd checked it out and it was OK but wouldn't be in the kitchen until tomorrow. I felt powerful. I was in the right.

"You must have some left over, I'll have that for now."

He didn't like it, there was no mistaking the vibes, but I stood my ground on the trampoline and he poured some out into my mug. Outside the door I could feel the sweat on me. The hotplate room had been like a stage, the fluorescent lights as hot and glaring as any stage lights.

Just before the landing screw banged me up, Scots Eddie with a precarious tower of food on his plastic plate came to tell me there was a movie on in the Rec after unlock. They would all be going. Then I was banged up and after the screw's final look through the spyhole I relaxed, felt a new kind of freedom. The trip went into a restful period. I listened to the football results, cared and didn't care. I ate some of the food slowly, each mouthful a little explosion, my slow chewing extracting taste and texture from each grain. I sipped the milk, a creamy waterfall in my mouth falling down and down.

It took a few minutes to come out of where I was and realise I'd been unlocked. I went out on the landing. There was no one about, but down on the Ones there was a big crowd at the main wing gates. There were shouts and jeers, the gates rocking under the weight of bodies like it was Highbury and the turnstiles were slow. I couldn't see any of my friends. The floor was bouncing through my feet. Some screws made a passage through the crowd and there was a big cheer as the gates were opened. I followed the crowd through and gave my name to another screw with a board. The Rec was only fifteen yards away but inside it was already dark. I couldn't see anyone and stumbled about till I found a chair near the back. The titles came up on the rolled-out screen, out of focus. Focus, focus you one-armed bastard, someone shouted out. After some false starts it came into focus to show THE FIXER. It sounded like some conspiracy movie in smoke-filled rooms. But no, on the screen appeared ST PETERSBURG 1910.

There were horses and carriages, cobbled and muddy streets. My head picked up the sound of horse bells: I could smell horse dung in the street. I was also in the Rec and could see pale faces all around me. Then on screen came a rich aristo lady, pale in the face, her face drawn tight with tension, hair drawn back tight. Against her better judgement she fancies a dark, curly-haired youth. A poor jew no doubt. A man of integrity, he rejects her and her face draws tighter still.

Next thing is she's accused him of rape and he's in some kind of jail. No messing about, wham-bang in the slammer. Shit. My heart was pounding. It's outrageous, how can anyone be so spitefully mean. Suddenly there's the voice of the interrogator, alternately wheedling and vicious. Oh I know that voice. "Don't say anything," I want to shout out. But I've got no voice.

It's a fifteen-round battle crammed into a few minutes of film. But your man does hold his ground. Now there's a cell on screen, a big one, a holding cell. Big figures loom up towards your man out of grey shadows. One of them gives him a real mean look: a psychopathic hulk: he's taunting your man. It's obvious, the interrogator has put him there deliberately. He wants to scare him shitless with some anti-semitic heavy. Then a bigger penny dropped. Never mind your man, what about me. I'm a new boy on the wing, it's dark and the wing is filled with psychos as well as professional criminals. Half and half from what I'm told. I'm sweating, wondering how the fuck I can get out. I cursed Scots Eddie. I was having a really good time on the wing, couldn't they have checked out the movie in advance, the storyline.

The acid is pumping around my veins, the rushes from my stomach less frequent but more unexpected when they do surge up strong as ever. Maybe it's good it is dark, no one can see me. I'm probably looking like a glint-eyed psycho myself, sweaty and tight-faced. I can feel the faces and bodies behind me, fuck knows what perverted villainy is going in those heads. I focus back on the screen, it can't be worse. No relief, looks as though your man is going to be ripped apart. Limb from limb. I remember Eddie this morning, light years away, I remember him telling me how the guy two cells down from me is a necrophiliac and me saying Don't give me the bollox, and then my disbelief melting away in face of the details till I'd surrendered, asked him to please shut up.

Thank Christ our man is suddenly on his own in a small cell. Then a smaller one. Never mind where I am, on the screen, claustrophobia writ large. They can't possibly put him in anything smaller. But they do. It's a cell like a sweat box in a paddy-waggon. He can just about stand up, but not straight, it's not high enough. He's unwashed and now he's got a beard and long. long hair. His eyes are black and immobile with a slight smile in his mouth. One moment it looks cretinous, then serene, then cretinous again.

I tell myself it's only a movie, they're getting paid for it, he's just an actor on a working day. Cut! Take One! The director giving instructions for Take Two, just make it that bit heavier. All in a days work on the set. Yes, and what are my mates doing, where the fuck are they? Why haven't I heard a scream from somewhere in the Rec? The fuckers aren't here, that's what it is. No wonder I haven't seen them. Probably decided not to come after all, that or they're so far out of it they couldn't even make it whereas as keen me, the freshman...

The scene switches. There's a pale faced priest in the corridor of the cell-block. Another tense, drawn face. Maybe he's the lady's brother, maybe her twin. He opens the cell door. Our man is having to stand in crucifixion pose. Is it going to be the last rites or a conversion job under duress. The priest sees your man. Silence. Then he screams, screams again, and faints. What's he seen, Christ crucified? The devil? I feel a beautiful rush of elation from the toes up. It's got so bad they can't touch him any more. They can't fucking touch him. They've done their worst.

It's an anti-climax when he's released after this. There's some other aristo, the Tsar maybe. Whoever it is, he's impressed with your man's story. His release becomes a big ceremony. A big shaft of doubt hits my brain, maybe the poor bastard is hallucinating himself, it's only a fantasy.

I don't know., it seemed real enough, the release. Be positive. Assume it's real. A good moral to the story. Hold on, don't admit anything. There may be places where it don't make a sods worth of difference, they'll kill you anyway but it's all you have going for you, don't admit anything.

As the lights went up I felt dazed and drained, had to make an effort to get out of the chair. There was a rush of cons. I still couldn't see anyone I knew, but as I got back to my cell I saw Scots Eddie coming out of it. His eyes were swollen and red, he'd been crying.

"Yes," I said. "I lived out every moment with the guy, through the mangle and out the other end."

He nodded and sat on the bed, quiet.

"I lost you all man, couldn't see anyone," I said, feeling bad that I'd had bad thoughts about my mates. "Still the guy made it. I mean he stuck by his guns and he made it."

"I know, I know" he said like he didn't quite believe it. We hugged each other.

MY PRODUCTIVE INPUT to PRINDUS, the work department of the prison network had been minimal. I'd never got to grips with those poxy wigwams. Being cack-handed is no virtue in the big free world but in prison, so what. From D Wing there were three shops which took

Category A men. I was allotted to the Master Tailors where cloth was cut for prison clothes, car seat covers, Lee Cooper jeans and Post Office uniforms. These were then sewn up in the Tailors shop upstairs. Whenever possible, clandestine cloth for our own tailored strides followed the same route. Now and then the screws would come down heavy on this business and on these same trousers and re-tailored shirts being carefully cleaned in the laundry, another shop which took Category A cons, the chaps. It was an important battle and the cons never gave way on the matter of personal laundry for themselves and others.

Category A cons had to have their own escort, clutching little red books in which our every movement was recorded. In the Master Tailors there were two or three discipline screws who sat around all day in case anything went off, and to give us a rub down on the way out. There were also two civvie instructors in white coats. They didn't know what to do with me and I found a place with Al the clerk con and Tony, a big hard looking guy out of South London. These were the chaps while the cons doing the cloth cutting were mostly nonces. Apart from Al filling in a couple of forms we did bugger all. Tony was half way through an eighteen stretch, a veteran of special wings which sounded like claustrophobic tranquility punctured by geezers stabbing their bridge partners over bad calls. Him and Al talked of mutual friends and stories of cock-ups we have known. There was Tony in the getaway car that ran out of petrol. Al came back with a tip-off he'd had on a bank messenger.

"I'm told he's carrying grands on this particular day so I've clocked his route and steamed in with a pick-axe handle. But he's held on to that fucking case like his life depends on it. By the time he's let go some have-a-go merchants are making themselves busy. Me and Alfie Sims had to club our way out of that lot."

"What do they get out of it, them people," Tony said. "A pat on the back, how's the head today and a mug shot in the papers."

"Beats me. Anyway after all that aggravation we're away. By the time we're back in the flop I'm thinking, Never mind, all's well that ends well. Only when I open the case what's in it, the geezer's fucking sandwiches, his sandwiches."

"What, smoked salmon?"

"Cheese and pickle as it happens."

Later Al started on about books we'd read and the run down of the London docks where he'd worked. It was no mystery, the bosses couldn't stomach the level of militancy. He said they'd finish off East London in the process.

When it came round to wage day me and Tony found we were paupers, just the bare minimum for half an ounce of Old H. Tony gave the Number Two civvie a pull. This one was a short, roly-poly Yorkshireman with a bluff and brass-tacks style that was bogus. He did not like Tony at all but was wary. Still, he got it across that we would continue on the bare minimum if we didn't work: no work, no smoke. I said we hadn't been offered a job. Which was how we came to have a stab at cutting car-seat covers out of mock lambswool. It involved clamping down eight pieces of the stuff with a pattern on top and Tony going to work with a power cutter.

We kept production to a steady trickle and spent most of the time over at Al's desk playing no-holes barred Scrabble. Come the next day and our wages were up by a pack of Rizla.

The Yorkshire civvie started talking quotas, Tony a transfer to the laundry. Yorkie said he could make a good job for himself here. Tony gave him a hard look. We went haywire with that cutter, gouges, tears and cut-off corners multiplied by eight. At best we gave rough approximations to a car-seat cover. Two days later Tony got his transfer to the laundry, Al got on full time classes and I inherited his post. There was not much work involved. Two or three invoices a day, counting bales of cloth now and then. The chief civvie, a quiet, elderly bloke took it all very seriously. He talked of Tolworth Towers, the PRINDUS HQ, in hushed tones. Tolworth must decide on this, he'd say. Or, This is how Tolworth want it done.

I read a lot but looked at the clock too much. It got worse when a Category A con turned up. The lies and bullshit that man talked! He'd done everything, been a racing driver, had his own ballroom, been a pilot, a commando. I gave up pulling him on the most glaring contradictions in his stories because he only made up even more elaborate lies to explain them away. Then there was the mystic. Too much.

Around this time a young Rasta with neat locks, name of Michael arrived on the wing. By this time I was well into the rhythm of the place, blase about what had first seemed like great freedom. One day I was coming down for breakfast when I picked up aggravation vibes. They came from just outside the sick-room opposite the hot plate room. There was young screw, also new on the wing, a square, fat pudding who was coming down heavy on Michael. I couldn't hear the words but I'll have you, you black cunt, that was the gist. Suddenly the screw's grabbed hold of Michael. Boom, Tony's jumped in. Hands on the screw. It's off. I moved in with around twenty other cons. The screw is surrounded and at that moment the PO, his ears tuned for aggravation, steps in, sorts it out. Cools things down, talks severely to Michael and the screw. The situation is simple: the PO doesn't have much control over personnel but he sure as hell doesn't want some young pig fucking up what is a relaxed wing. No one got nicked and it all fell into place, how the PO was the same one who'd taken me on the Holloway escort, whereas the uptight screw who wanted D wing screwed down, him I'd hardly ever seen on the wing. Probably on the borstal wing throwing his weight around.

It was hard to admit but I had a certain respect for the pragmatic PO. On the other hand his control over the wing was not total, the Wing Governor was a hard-liner and there was some selective aggravation especially from one screw, Phillips. This Phillips was not new on the wing but was a pig of a screw. He was one of those with the peak of his cap close to vertical, coming straight down to cut his nose in half. Possibly an ex-redcap, probably ex-Wandsworth. Maybe he filed down that peak but his stomach was out of control, bulging over his belt.

Early in 1974 when Mr Heath decreed Switch Off Something the screws were having a gas by doing their bit, switching off cell-lights almost immediately after bang-up. A few of us attempted to refuse bang-up in protest but it never caught on. It was not important enough to most cons and the only result was a few nickings. Meanwhile Phillip's was on his own mission, getting on Mick's back which didn't take much working out, it was because Mick was Irish. Sure he'd knocked off some Post Offices but then screws don't get worked up about where you get your dough. He was simply a 100% sound con and Irish. I reckoned they knew that a lot of Irish Republican prisoners were in the pipeline for long-term wings. Maybe that was too elaborate and conspiratorial but Phillips was the screw who'd be first to pick up on hints that certain aggravation would be in order. Down to him, Mick had already been down the block a couple of times.

He made a point of getting posted on Mick's end of the Threes. His latest stroke was to make a big show of rattling his keys as he did the unlocking, then missing out Mick's cell, finding some new rule each time to keep him locked up.

Mick was a guy we all liked, not just because he was great for the crack and a dab hand at Kalooki. We tried pulling Phillips about it verbally. He would either do a strong-and-silent number or repeat the same obscure rule over and over.

It was just a matter of time before Mick gave him a dig. That might have been OK but we also knew that Timmy Noonan and others who'd been involved in the Parkhurst riot were still getting stick seven years after.

One evening when he was unlocked we gave up the Kalooki to plan some action that might change the situation. It was Peter came up with the idea. It fitted the bill, couldn't be pinned on anyone if we did it right, though it did depend on the gossip in the place getting the word around that it was down to Phillips without it going further than that. The action would hit a lot of screws and it was naive to think they'd be queuing up to slag off Phillips, but we hoped questions would be asked.

D Wing was built in the traditional style with around eighty single cells to each landing. Half way along the Ones next to the Wing gates there was a control-box which housed a tannoy and a Glaswegian SO with a permanent cold. There was also the traditional diamond patterned safety wire running the length of the wing, stretched across it from one side of the Twos to the other. At some point those in control of the wing had been pragmatic or cons had insisted on it, either way thick polythene sheeting had been placed along the safety wire. This covered the area under which there were eating tables, leaving the wire bare at either end of the Wing and in the middle above the control box. It made for a perpetual twilight on the Ones but prevented dust and pigeon shit falling into cons' dinners.

Over the next couple of days we helped London Eddie stash the necessary supplies that he had access to. The morning we were ready we ate our porridge in Eddie's cell.

"You're sure Mick's down on the Ones for everyone to see," Peter asked.

"He's there," I said. "It's gutting him missing out on it but I told him, there's no point putting himself on offer."

"Yes, but is he there."

"Fucks sake Peter, he's there. We can't hold his hand."

We took five minutes to package the material, Eddie standing guard outside his cell as we did it. When we were finished I went out along the landing to the top of one staircase, Peter to the other. There was the usual rush hour, life in the bee-hive. Then came the familiar voice like you could hear the snot dripping, DOWNSTAIRS FOR LABOUR.

DOWNSTAIRS FOR LABOUR.

We waited.

Over the next two minutes the screws for each labour party assembled round the control box. Cons started to group around the Wing gate. I looked along the Threes. Eddie was standing in his doorway. The Threes landing screw in his glass cage was facing the other way listening to the life story of a parole-punter. I gave the thumbs up, looked along the landing again and saw Peter do the same.

The two Eddies burst out of the cell and ran about fifteen yards along the landing till they were above the Control box. They ran as fast as anyone could carrying a polythene bag full of a few pints of white gloss paint. They heaved the bags over the railings. Splat! The bags crashed on to the safety wire and split. Glass shot out and spewed over the group of screws. We didn't have time to look at them cop it but dumped the original paint cans in the recess, split up and walked to different cells on the Threes and then came out again and down to the Ones as if going to work. There was plenty of running about afterwards but no more than that, we'd left no paint stains on the landing.

It had been a tight operation, no known grasses in sight. Besides which the glossed-up screws were out of action. It took them two hours to re-organize themselves; two hours of gloating or indifference from the cons; two hours late for work; two hours of lost labour time to amend PRINDUS accounts at Tolworth Towers. Of course there was plenty of ranting and raving from the screws, the whole of D Wing was in line for castration.

Mick didn't get any more aggravation but there was plenty of gossip. Three weeks later he was shanghaied to Wandsworth, the standard unofficial punishment. We had a post-mortem. It didn't look so wonderful, out of the frying pan and into the fire. The screws had one too. The upshot of theirs was that they got an even longer length of polythene which stretched the entire length of the wing without gaps. We had a laugh about that when we heard Mick was OK and on his way to Maidstone.

AT AROUND THIS TIME a whole table on the Ones became vacant. We decided we'd like a spell of eating out and organized ourselves as a table. We were joined by Harry, a sharp young mod from Hoxton. I'd seen him in C Wing, confident hustler and the leading light in a mob-handed attack on a screw with a sharpened broom handle. He also came on like a racist. Strange, none of us were looking for aggravation but some part of us knew that with Harry it was always on the cards. But then worrying about the months and years ahead was unreal, so what the fuck. There was also Steve, another young long-hair in the cell above mine, next to Eddie on the Threes. We got on OK only for him falling asleep with the arm on over his record-player. It was always 'Tubular Bells'. I detested 'Tubular Bells'. Now and then I'd try banging the roof of my cell with a broomstick. More often I'd turn up my radio for John Peel who never let me down in five years.

There were ten or so eating tables on the Ones. There were also two black and white TVs positioned towards either end of the wing next to the staircases. Our table was at the far end from Table Four which was for the chaps, the Train Robbers and some other heavy guys. Next to us was another chaps table. Between us and table Four was a table-tennis set-up, a snooker table and four other tables. Table Six was made up of seven or eight black cons. We played a lot of table-tennis. The snooker table was nearly-monopolized by a train robber and a sharp-talking black American con. Nearly everyone else played Kalooki but Table Six was for dominos, a loud, rhythmic ballet. Dudes danced around the table slamming down dominos on cue. Harry went on about them being noisy and flash.

"You've got some fucking front," we'd say. "You're not exactly a doormouse yourself."

"Yeah but they stick together, they make themselves into a firm, they're the most prejudiced of all."

"So they're into the same things, you don't play dominos."

"With all that fucking noise, all that bloodclart and rasclart, you're joking."

"You sound like a screw, you just don't like people being cheerful."

"It's not that."

But Harry was also having the crack with Josh, an athletic black con who was as sharp as Harry.

"If I'm from the jungle man, where the fuck is Hoxton?"

It's a tiny village of mud flats that got lost between Islington and Hackney," Peter said.

"And full of grasses," Eddie said.

"You what," Harry shouted, tensing up. "Are you calling me a fucking grass."

Eddie stayed cool. "You know I'm not calling you a grass, otherwise we wouldn't be eating on the same table, but your manor is full of them, it's probably why you're here."

"So what's Lewisham then, that's if you can fucking find it, one hundred percent sound people are they?"

Josh was pissing himself. "You want to come up Stoke

Newington when you is out and about, safer up there."

"What with all them shebeens and blues, fuck that."

"Worse noise down your way, people stabbing and shooting each other, the jungle am safer."

I'd got my flute and harmonica in by then and was playing a lot with Al on guitar and Eddie drumming on a bucket or his own guitar. Scots Eddie did some singing on and off. We rotated the cells we played in, but Saturday night was the big night. First we'd eat, curry or pasta. This involved buying some stuff from the official canteen out of wages and some investments with a weight-lifting freak who was a big noise in the kitchen. That got us the meat we could build around. I enjoyed doing the cooking. It was a rare chance to make something; it was a taste of ordinary life. What's more the kitchen felt like free territory, we could block the doors when it was needed. An area of free expression like for the Lebanese con who'd unzip his flies and slap his cock down on a work surface and shout a curse if his cooking was interrupted.

After eating we'd make for one of our own cells. These were getting to be like shebeens themselves as Josh told Harry. They were largely teetotal, true but there was nearly always something to smoke. A black con called Mo made the odd appearance on drums, usually in search of a spliff.

"Here he is, on the ponce again," Harry would say, less venom by the week.

"Me man, I'm just trying to stop you boys getting too heavy into this here drug."

"You've got a big heart Mo."

"I know man, it's the source of all my troubles, but it's here to stay," he said, launching into a soft, driving rhythm on an upturned plastic bucket. He stopped only when the spliff came round.

"Your taste in weed am improving."

"Cheeky sod."

Around May 1974 I got excited when Labour won the election, one which the miners had brought about. Who rules the country, Mr Heath had asked. And got an answer. I thought maybe this time the spongy British state would not be able to keep all the contradictions under wraps. But in no time at all there was talk of private armies and coups. A secret fear, that if the wrong side won any bust-up, they'd introduce internment surfaced. My head was in and out of the everyday life of D Wing. One day when my head was definitely not in it I was out on lunchtime exercise with Eddie and Harry. We'd got tired of the drab round the asphalt walk and found a sun-trap by the Rec. After a while we heard an outbreak of noise on the wing followed by some unusual screw activity by the wing gates. Exercise continued. Fine-tuned internal clocks told us it was running late. A couple of minutes later Winston, a black con came out of the wing doors with a two-screw escort. Nicked. Soon after one of the young white hopefuls off of Table Ten came out the same way.

Odds-on, a fight. It was another ten minutes before we were taken in. The wing seemed normal enough, the usual queue of cons at the hotplate entrance.

I asked Steve what had gone down. It had been like this. A few days before a young black lifer with a constant high-voltage energy had blacked the eye of a quiet white con called Colin. It had been generally seen as a bit of a liberty. Fights were neither frequent nor exceptional, the normal thing would have been for Colin or his mates to make a come-back. This time it had been taken out of his hands. Some cons were saying, The blacks are getting too pushy, Steve said. I'd been well out wing life not to have heard this bullshit. The shock was greater when I heard it was Tony, the hard nut who'd defended Michael and who I'd worked with, was at the heart of it, plotting up to make a chair leg job of it. In the event it had blown up this lunchtime but had been only verbals and a couple of punches. Winston and the other face had been picked out at random. A disinterested source off Table Four confirmed it was Tony was at the heart of it. He said Tony was cracking up, had attacked his young best pal only the week before.

On the Saturday night we had a great jam. Mo dropped in with a pal of his, a guy I'd argued with over his taste for Gistaldesic. Mostly I'd go sick and score him one when he asked but then I'd refused. A bit self-righteous maybe, there were times when I'd have liked to be spark out. But we made good music that night, six scat singers on top of the harp, Peter's sharp chord changes and Mo and Eddie on drums.

Banged up later in my cell it was a different story. I thought about what it would have been like if I had known what was going down on the wing; if I'd known about this plotting up to Teach the blacks a lesson. What then? Who was I? I had a certain respect but was marginal, still a bit of a weirdo. What would I have done, talked it out with Tony? Slugged it out? Sobering up fast from the music I wondered how long I'd have survived as a white leftist in an American jail, San Quentin, Attica. A day? A couple of weeks? I was not so tough and it seemed like even if you were very tough you'd go down in the end. I remembered a white Weatherman who'd been in such a situation, Sam Melville. A guy who had broken some barriers and slugged it out to the end. Murdered in Rockefeller's massacre at Attica; Rockefeller who was supposed to represent the unacceptable face of liberalism in the Republican Party.

Maybe this line of thinking was ludicrously self-important. Why should what I did or thought make any difference. Good any way that Harry was not involved, he was a changed man. Still, what would I have done if I had known. I got up, I laid down and the thoughts went round and round. If Steve put on Tubular Bells I would scream. I wished I was free.

The World Cup came round. The Dutch team were a

revelation, playing football from another planet, football that had always seemed to be possible but had never happened. I argued the toss with Mo who supported Brazil like all the other guys off the dominos table.

"Brazil aren't like they used to be," I said. "They're playing like Europeans now whereas the Dutch have gone beyond all that shit."

"Brazil, dancers man and the best of them are black dancers."

"It's a dictatorship man, Brazil. Run by white generals. What's the life expectancy for black people there?"

"You giving me that political shit again man, always that political shit."

Most of the games started an hour or so before bang-up. The Scotland-Yugoslvia game was a cracker. Bang-up time came around with about twenty five minutes to go. A screw pulled out the plug from the wall socket by table Four. A leading face from the table put it back in again. It was a shock. This guy didn't want trouble, he was in line for a big chunk of parole at some point. For the first couple of minutes it was impossible to get back into the drama of the game, more electric in the wing than the stadium in Germany. There must have been a hundred of us around the screen and we were joined by the crowd from the other TV. The football was exciting again. Half of Table Four were grouped around the plug, the screws were not making a move. Just before full time the Wing Governor turned up with a two-screw escort, a thin faced bastard in the regulation tweed jacket. From the staircase he threatened this that and the other while the laid-back PO looked on.

Around the end of August there was a minor scandal, a young Welsh con was shanghaied.

"Caught him at it didn't they," Eddie said.

"What?"

"With that Campion on the twos."

"What the fuck are you talking about?"

"He was bang at it, pumping away in the kid."

"You're saying that in all-male, long-term institution, homosexuality is so out of order they shanghai people?"

"It's in the rules somewhere."

This was surely besides the point. "Well what do they fucking expect," I asked.

"They don't expect fucking," Eddie said laughing. "Anyway do you fuck blokes?"

"As it happens, no. I mean you're good-looking yourself but I don't fancy you."

He blushed then said coolly, "Well that's lucky."

It didn't occur to me to ask why it was the young guy'd been shanghaied and not Campion. Eddie just said he was mad about it, cursing the screws. I could see his point even when Eddie said all the love affairs he'd seen in the jail were between an older face and a youth. Power relationships he said, with lots of bullshit sentiment. It seemed harsh, I wasn't so confident about the purity of my sentiments. I'd become an expert wanker, I'd got to know my body well and everything it liked. A good one could last an hour. Other times it would be routine, like lots of the roll-ups I smoked, and I'd end up feeling more speedy and wound-up. At the time I had the bollock-ache with it and was abstaining. Saving it up for a rainy day, Eddie said. I said I was a bit afraid that playing so much with images and fantasies would blight any real emotions.

"It's an occupational hazard," Eddie said with a shrug. "Anyway don't worry about it, just wait till you're out there in bed with a real woman, no problem, smashing. Your problem is you see worries everywhere."

At this time he had three months to do and me four years, but he was right, I spent too much time worrying about things

I could do very little about.

By this time our table had developed into some kind of force, a bit far-out but not so marginal anymore. It was helped by the drug revolution. Heavies who'd previously seen hash and weed as a debilitating force that would somehow reduce their dignity, sharpness and effectiveness were turned on by the stuff itself. In this area we had a good name as quality testers who knew the score, and as efficient smugglers. At the same time there the end of an era on the cards. Peter and Eddie were well on the way out while the table got new inputs from other jails, Malcolm shanghaied from Gartree with whom I read Karl Marx's 'Capital' chapter by chapter, and Julian from Crumlin Road Belfast where he'd been the jew in the rooftop demonstration of catholics, protestants and one jew, 'common' criminals demanding better conditions. There was a story to it I heard for the first time, how there had been two demonstrations, the first a success, the second a disaster, the army sent in to loose off plastic bullets on the wing. He showed me a scarred Old H tin that had saved him from the impact. And how had this second demo come about? How, because one guy with heroic aspirations but who had bottled out of the first rooftop demo could not live with having bottled out, and pushed and pushed for a second, the one too many, that they all knew was one too many.

More dramatically Gerard came on the wing and our table Nine. He'd been done on the Old Bailey bombing and was the first of the Irish Republicans to appear on the Wing. He'd been on hunger strike in the hospital wing, demanding to do his life sentence in the north of Ireland, and I'd managed to make some contact through an exceptional redband who was far from being a parole-punter. It had got to the point where me and Eddie were going to go on hunger strike in support even though we didn't believe in it as a tactic because it seemed to assume that the other side were ultimately humane people.

Hours before we were due to start we heard that Gerard had won his demand. Man, was I relieved.

His arrival put new life into us, he didn't approve the dope smoking but was an enthusiast drummer. We went out with bang. After nearly a year of playing me and Peter had it pretty tight, and when Brian who'd been a pro guitarist on the out arrived, the music took off. We found out there were prizes awarded to cons for artistic endeavor, including music, awarded on behalf of Arthur Koestler. There was also a sympathetic teacher who had access to amps and speakers.

Using the Koestler awards as a prop we started to hassle an AG for access to this gear. We are serious people, we said, it involves being recorded by local radio and we don't want to make an unrehearsed shambles of it. We blinded him with sound talk and on the strength of it ended up doing gigs in the Rec for all the wings with the help of a great drummer off of C Wing. Of course our egos were in full swing but after a shaky start there was the great sound of stamping feet. The Rec was shaking as we moved into the final number, a version of The Velvet Underground's Sister Ray. The screws were signalling us to stop but it couldn't be. There hadn't been such a night since Kathy Kirby had started a third comeback in the same venue, made to feel like a queen by all the East London faces who'd known her in better times, grabbing at her dress, cheering. She'd risen to it. I knew how she felt. On the last round of Sister Ray, telling Cecil how he shouldn't shoot the sailor with his new piece on account of how it would stain the carpet I was hoarse, kaput, out of it.

IT WAS GOOD TIMING, two weeks later and Peter was out with a celebration. From then on, things didn't stop happening and that without night after night in the cell; eating the same shit day in and out; dead hours of Kalooki and table-tennis. Most of all it was different because I'd got a stake in an escape project far more realistic than the C Wing tunnel.. It removed me from much interest in the Wing. However it panned out, it would mean the end of what we'd had collectively. I felt bad about not being able to tell Eddie and Harry, we'd been through a lot together. I had a sort of dread of seeing Harry's face the moment we went for it. I found it hard to stay involved in conversations that had till then kept me sane.

But the Wing would not go away. It was fucking perverse, how things kept happening as we accumulated the wherewithal for the escape. It began with Harry being cut up by a head-banger in front of the TV. Harry was Table Nine so Table Nine had to do something. Of course we had to be the minders and look-outs for his comeback and of course Harry had to go right over the top and I kidded myself there'd be no consequences just because he'd left it a couple of weeks.

Within ten days Malcolm and a face from Table Ten, both involved in the escape, were shanghaied. It left just three of us, Gerard and a cheerful, resourceful face off Table Ten. We couldn't understand it, surely we'd been grassed but they hadn't rumbled our equipment. Then one morning I went to Eddie's cell for breakfast. The door was locked. There was no cell card. I lifted the spy-hole flap. The cell was empty, like he'd never been there at all. He had only two months to go, had not known of the escape. The penny dropped. It was Harry's comeback, Table Nine as hoodlums.

And there was no let up. A huge culchie screw made a rare appearance on the wing, evening overtime away from his normal bortsal wing where he could throw his weight around. On D Wing it didn't go down so well. He tried to stop a black con and another guy we knew from going to the gym. They stood their ground. The culchie screw struck out. That was it. He was poleaxed by Freddie Foreman, the heaviest con on Table Four, a guy due out on Home Leave the next day. They were all nicked and in minutes we had sit-downs with barricades around the TV sets. Bang-up time came and no one moved. On Table Four negotiations began and finally the word came down to cool it, Freddie would get his Home Leave.

No let up. Bam, the Birmingham pub bomb went off. It sounded worse by the minute. Gerard got heavy looks, there were whispers of threats, threats and rumours by the minute.

With some heavy Irish blaggers we put it about that he would get plenty of backing if it went off. Nothing went off except the best tailor of trousers on the wing who threatened mayhem to the IRA bastard then refused to make Gerard a pair of strides. That was a drag, he'd need some if we made it over the wall.

No let up at all. News came through that a con on C wing had been murdered by screws in the block, beaten to pulped pulp then hanged to cover it up, a suicide story. It seemed too cynically brutal to be true. I knew screws could be brutal but this was too much, all my deepest fears congealed. The next day con witness reports came through. It was unavoidable, true. The pragmatic PO's last act before losing out the power struggle to the Wing Governor was to refuse to have one of the implicated screws on our wing. No getting away from it, escape or no escape, something had to be done. Table Nine was approached about doing a petition. We were sceptical, petitions, they usually ended up as toilet paper. I'd never heard of cons being listened to when it mattered, not till the events were long over and rendered safe by time. But this con said he could guarantee it would get in the national papers and the mood in the wing was that it would get total support. The project was straightforward, get close to every name on that paper, stash it over night and smuggle it out before it was grassed up. We undertook jobs one and two. It worked.

Nothing else could happen. The shanghais had been down

to Harry, the escape hadn't been grassed, there'd been no turnovers that got near our equipment. On the Friday night with a week to go till we were ready I stayed awake late even though it was early bang-up night. I was too gee'd up for easy sleep. Gee'd up, no idea of what I was going to do if we made it but wanting it, wanting out of all this. I knew it was early when I was awoken by the sound of the door opening. A security PO was stood there with two side kicks.

"Pack your kit," he said.

Half an hour later I was in Reception, limbo. D Wing was a closed story I was no longer part of. Just like that.

CHANGE OF SCENERY

IT WAS NOT just like that. I thought about my friends on the Wing, thought about them and felt sad. My face set in a hard mask. Harder as we drove out of west London as the unknown PO told me I wouldn't be allowed my record-player, not where I was going. He told me several times. I thought about the escape, so near but so far. It was a grey November Saturday afternoon. The van was in convoy, cop car in front, cop car behind.

We were on the A40. Deduction by elimination limited only by my road geography. I knew which were the max security jails. Wakefield, Hull; we weren't going there. Parkhurst and Albany on the island, we weren't going there. Somewhere early on, the Uxbridge Road, I'd asked where we ere going. A moment of weakness.

"You'll find out when you get there," the PO'd said. The wise guy. It could only be Gartree or Long Lartin, the two newest security jails. When I saw the sign for Oxford I knew it had to be L-L. It was a name.

We crossed a county boundary. The leading cop car went off a slip road, another slid on to take its place. Smooth. The state was well financed. In the custom-built minibus with the standard blackened windows the screws talked about overtime and their social club. On and on they talked about some binge in the club. How many pints was it the PTI had drunk? We veered off through evenly spaced picture postcard villages, Chipping this and Chipping that. Alien territory.

Soon the villages were gone. The screws were livening up. We drove across flat land. I saw a bland but weird-looking set of walls, a comprehensive school with barbed wire topping and tall floodlights. Long Lartin obviously.

The wing was weird too, E Wing they called it. It was small, modern, closed in. The scene around the hotplate was quiet. Straight away I missed the street-market rush of the Scrubs. Not that I felt so lively. I banged up with some tea feeling wooden. This was the sticks, these modern-looking buildings and floodlights in the middle of nowhere. Maybe it was just the bustle of D Wing but I'd always felt I was in London in the Scrubs.

Sat with my tea at a small table I looked out the window. It was well-barred but large and well positioned. By the cell door there was a panel set into the wall with indicator lights and buttons. A screw had explained that by following the correct sequence of buttons I could get out at night for a shit. Night sanitation they called it. The heating worked, all to the good, just looking out into the grey outside made me shiver. Clean and comfortable the cell looked but as I ate my tea the smallness of it made itself felt. Mostly the ceiling was low, no more than seven foot high. Seven foot square the floorspace. A cube, a bland cube painted in grey and brown speckle. My old home, the one I'd woken up in that very morning had wound up as a fait accompli of orange, pink and blue. All done in a night with some contraband paint from Eddie. In this place the light too was dull, boxed away in a frosty, partially transparent casing screwed to the ceiling. I got the shivers again, it was in asylum mode with a ceiling that bore down. They would have had architects on the job, wicked bastards, weekly conferences with Home Office psychologists as they drew up their plans. I could do without the de luxe shitting service but did not want to live in a box.

On evening association I saw no one I knew, no one took any notice of me and I wasn't in the mood for talking. Later my depression changed tack. I forgot about the cell, what hurt was the prospect of escape being snatched away. For six weeks I'd lived with the possibility of being free and during this time had stepped through a door from it as a fantasy to believing in it is a real and realistic project. From that moment we'd worked bit by bit to make it real. I thought about a woman on the out I loved, the possibility of touch, eye-contact, smell, and stopped wanking. Now it was all in my head again, securely fastened inside. I fell asleep grinding my teeth. It was going to require a real effort to find the enthusiasm to fight for things like my record-player.

There was an item of kit-issue that was new to me, a shapeless grey overcoat. Essential too I found out on the Sunday afternoon exercise. I followed a couple of greycoats down lengths of identical corridor and came out on a large grass field. The perimeter wall and inner fence stretch about five hundred yards either way. There were football posts, rugby posts, cameras and screws with dogs scattered around the fence. It was freezing, a cold wind blowing across the plain or the vale as they called it, the vale of fucking Evesham. Two wings back onto the field, the cells on the Ones looked cosy.

There were only a score or so of cons out on the field. A brummie guy caught up with me. Long Lartin was the nearest Security nick to Birmingham. I learned a few other things too; there were six wings in all for about 70 cons each and four of them were open. What were we, pioneers. That we were paid in coins, fifty and ten pence pieces. That everyday lunchtime exercise was on the asphalt yard the other side of the wing blocks but that we had the field for weekends and in the summer, for some evenings. Then the brummie guy said I could do well for myself in this place.

"Oh yes."

"It's a good time now, coming up to Christmas, you'd be surprised."

I waited, wishing the cunt would get to the point. The cold was attacking my ears, drilling in.

"Whoever you're making the soft toy for see, whoever it is can hand it out on a visit to his kids and pretend he's made it himself. You see what I mean and I'm not just talking teddy-bears, you need a wider range."

I looked at him wary. Maybe this was an asylum, the bastards. Waves of regret for the Scrubs came on and I could see myself winding up like the Armley-freak who'd done Jim's head in back in Brixton. I stayed silent wanting to give him a nudge, say to him man to man, Fuck the soft toys, What's the crack like.

I was glad to get back to the warmth of the cell and look over the wing. Not only was it small, the three floors were linked by just the one staircase. You could see the architects at work, plotting all their lines to the end of isolating cons into small groups, keeping control. Each landing was divided into two spurs with six cells on either side. At the half way point there were larger spaces at right angles to the spurs. On one side there were recesses. On the Ones the space on the opposite side contained the hotplate and a tiny kitchen for cons, behind that offices for the PO, the SO, and the Welfare. On the Twos there were two TV rooms, and on the Threes a small 'games room' that contained one table for cards. I was on the Twos again in one of the Cat A cells where the bed was bolted to wall and floor, and the bars were said to be tougher.

While I was giving it the once over, a London face I'd met briefly in the Scrubs when he was in transit said hello. He said the jail was a doddle and that it would soon fill up with a better class of con. He mentioned another con he thought I might like. He did it with real gentility, did not say, He's a bit of an odd-ball like yourself, just that I might like him. So I went to David's cell and met a great friend. It felt familiar, stepping in his cell, books, papers and clothes all over the place. He soon had my head spinning with ideas he was working on: the nature of time; the changing economic function of imprisonment; an existential view of theft and the night. For the brain at least this place would be no graveyard. He also told me a bit of his story, how he'd been through the works. Orphanage, approved school, borstal, prison.

Christmas came around. I spent it down the block. In the Scrubs I'd had an outside teacher for an hour a week to help with an Economics degree I was doing. As it happened he was based in London and Oxford and was willing to continue. Here they blanked him. I got mad, partly it was losing something valuable, mostly an immediate hatred of the Education Officer who had a soft, bearded, sincere appearance and a small, mean heart. I blanked the course and refused labour in the Tailor's shop where I was working. The block was a concentrated version of the whole place. On its entry door it said SEGREGATION UNIT. I gave up my shoes and got a pair of plastic slippers. The cell was bare except for a low bed and pisspot and the block built around a small exercise yard. It was quiet, the inner sanctum of the larger segregation unit of Long Lartin. There was only one other con down there, Dennis, a fifty year old recidivist who was far from being an old lag. His eyes sparkled and he set a furious pace round the twenty by ten yards on our two dobs of daily exercise. His story came in clipped sentences with no change of tone, not even in the final miles of the motorway chase that ended up with him nicked.

On Christmas Eve the Governor came round. He wore a

tweed jacket with matching cap. Speaking to me man to man he suggested I go back on the Wing for Christmas. I had made my point, he would look into the matter. It was a season of goodwill, why suffer needlessly. His interests were obvious, they'd have to staff the block over the holiday period just for two cons. I told him to fuck off.

Asking what cons are in for was considered bad form, even why they're down the block. Dennis had opened up on both scores so I asked him why he was on Governor's 43. This was not Rule 43 for sex-cases or debtors, for your own protection It was more like a conspiracy rap without the trial: the Governor thinks you're a threat to the Good Order And Discipline of the jail and that's it, bang, down the block.

"So why don't they like you?"

"My best pal, Tony, was on an escape. Nearly made it. They had me down for making the jack. Tony was ghost-trained."

"But the Governor wanted you up now?"

"I told him why now. No."

We did get our exercise come the day itself and the screws were not frothing at the mouth. Overtime? They loved it and this would be what, double, treble time? Dennis asked me about a con in the Tailor's shop, a guy of his own age, what did I think of him. I saw him as a dapper, well-spoken Scottish gay guy. Dennis had known him a long time on and off, in one nick or another.

"He's got bitter and twisted," he said.

I pictured him again and couldn't see it which, as it happened, did not say much for my perception.

"Rose-coloured spectacles," Dennis said. "Throw them away. Got to see people as they are."

"What do you suggest, shades," I said.

The dinner tray weighed three times the normal. I didn't eat much, not sure my stomach could cope. I thought about Dennis and his mate, the nearly successful escape. This was obviously no dummy's nick. But I'd also found out a few days before that Gerard's attempt had failed. He'd been on top of the wall as the cop cars screamed across Scrubs Common, the cops with their shooters out. Ian had fallen off the ladder, slowed it down, even so the cops had been fast, faster than we'd ever envisaged. And this place here, I didn't know the local terrain and it would take at least nine months to know who was who to work out anything remotely realistic.

Then I'd only have two and a bit to go. The moment I gave up on the Christmas pud I reconciled myself to doing another three years four months.

Just before the nicking I'd got a letter from a woman I loved very much. We'd not communicated since the trial, one or two of our supporters had got very self-righteous, saying Els had been out of order over some business of a photograph and money and I, prig of prigs, had gone along with it. The letter had come out of the blue. It was long and loving. It made me very happy and I wrote back straight away. I longed to see her again.

I was back on the Wing just before New Year. I wished I had not bothered. There was a letter from my mum, Els was dead. She'd been in Holland for Christmas and caught two viruses at once. Twentyseven years old and not able to breathe in a hospital in her own country that she didn't much like. I read the letter over and over looking for loopholes, for some mis-reading. There were no loopholes. It was grey monochrome cold outside. It would be cold in Holland, she was dead and frozen under the ground.

The cell door clicked open. The tannoy boomed out.
DOWNSTAIRS FOR OUTSIDE ASSOCIATION
DOWNSTAIRS FOR OUTSIDE ASSOCIATION
I walked down the corridors, the robot. Walked round the field. Round and round and round. I didn't want to stop walking. Not ever.

There was something else, something I didn't want to think about.

I was the last one off the field, shepherded in by a posse of screws. The letter was still on the table back in my cell. I knew what it was going to say. Els had gone to Holland two or three days before Christmas, that's what she'd said she was going to do, there was no way she could have got my letter posted to London. No way that she'd ever know I'd been silly, blanking her like that with my disgusting self-righteousness. No way of thanking her for her generous letter. No way of knowing that I'd thought of her so much in that time.

Another voice cut in, what a self-absorbed fucking bastard I was. Why was my letter so important. My letter. My letter.

Because it's important, it matters to me.

To you, yes it matters to you, what about her.

Tears snaked their way around the fortifications of front and slid out. I re-read her letter through the blur, my heart standing still. It was so happy, generous, optimistic, she'd really made something for herself and then taken the effort to write to the hero toerag who'd given nothing but cold silence.

I was curled up in a corner on the bed the waves of self-disgust frighteningly strong. I tried to turn then to anger. But there was no hit-and-run driver, no aeroplane where costs had been cut, no psychotic killer, no selfish killer. Viruses were fucking viruses and I had been a prig.

There was no way around it, I was everything leftists were accused of, what I'd accused leftists of myself, I was a fucking prig who had not written because. Because clauses one, two and three.

For the next weeks I lived off routine. Went to work, came back from work and spent most of my free time with David but I couldn't talk about Els with him or anyone else. The one decent doctor I'd come across in the Scrubs described depression as an extreme case of sadness. It was all a waste and if there was no way of seeing it at as anything else, that's what it was.

Two things lifted me out of this extreme sadness. Number one, Gerard turned up on my wing, a ball of energy after two or three months in the Scrubs chokey. I could hardly believe it, on the same wing. They'd put him in the chokey after the escape attempt. He and Ian were both lifers, remission hadn't entered into it. He didn't know and probably never would, he said, if those few seconds lost when Ian had fallen off the ladder would have made any difference.

And here he was on F wing. Him and David. We couldn't stop talking. It was good to be talking again. Gerard had this wonderful combination of open-mindedness and purposeful determination and we examined the newspapers for each day news of Portugal as keenly as any Portuguese emigre. Something truly exciting was happening there, in a vaccuum when it came to the usual centres of power, people were making their own decisions and re-shaping their own lives. We had a sense even then that the forces which constitute capitalist and superpower reality and assert themselves as the only possible reality would at some point come down heavy on this revolution but it was inspiring all the same.

Gerard arrived with all his energy and one night I met Els in a dream. It was somewhere I'd never been among mountains. I knew she was dead but did not want to ask. I mustn't have felt guilty after all or it was she who waved away any need for explanations with her throaty laugh I knew so well. She was saying things, not speaking: why did I look so glum; how I always took things too serious.

They must have realized they'd made a cock-up. One afternoon I was pulled out of the workshop for a cell-spin. Instead they moved me next door to F Wing under protest. Not long afterwards resistance was rewarded and Gerard was flown to the Kesh.

THE RAT

F WING WAS LIVELIER and Els's death a duller everyday pain. I already knew George from the Tailors shop, a Scots con who had been a pal of Jake's in Gartree. He was a cheerful guy who said he was bisexual and could run off a well-fitting set of strides in no time. On the wing he was part of a little Scots firm who introduced me to Billy Connolly and then complained about the translation work they had to do. It was the usual mix on the wing, lifers, nonces, some chancers, working criminals and some faces from Birmingham, London and Liverpool. Some I respected, some were full of shit, coups they'd pulled off that always ran into telephone numbers but good boys in the jail.

The Twos spur I was on got to be sound. Phil, a tasty guy from Birmingham, who ran the book on the wing, was already there when arrived. Likewise the Harrier. They had him down as anti-social, having as little to do with screws as possible. He had resolved never to enter the TV room, had a severe haircut, and motivated me into fitness running, with sometimes sarcasm, enthusiasm now and then. There was also the Sailor, a big, gentle scouser who was in patches for a while as well as being on the book. Patches were yellow stripes down your trousers and black and white targets sewn on the back of the jacket. It meant he had escaped, been caught at it or been accused of trying. He had in fact been on the run for a few years and was a fine ballad singer and hooch-maker.

Most of all Irish republican prisoners slowly filtered through from the allocation prisons. On to F wing came Joe, another great friend, a souped-up, street-wise twenty year old from Irish Birmingham. He looked lost the first couple of days then opened up, an expert at setting off Alarm bells which were situated all over the jail and were there for screws in trouble. He would set them off and the heavy-mob would rush round the corridors and look dead stupid when they arrived at an empty space. If there was time we'd find a discreet vantage point and look out for which screws looked ready to spew up from the exercise. Sometimes there's be a rash of bell-ringing and the Governor would put up notices on the lines of A Small Minority Spoiling It For The Majority. He did love a notice, that man. You'd have thought the jail was a fucking Outward Bound course. Joe's arrival and the coming of summer cheered me up no end. We started to get regular evening exercise on the field which also meant time to see Dave who was still on E wing and who I missed.

THE SUN IS WARM and light through the cell window. It comes through the spaces between bars and lays stripes of light on me, lying on a bright striped blanket. It throws up shadows on wall and ceiling, the shadows of bars ballooned at off-beat angles.

I'm thinking about this pavement I know, a good one with big slabs that warm up in the sun, slanting unevenly down towards a basement. Maybe not thinking about it, more a case of it arriving just at a bad moment when even life outside had seemed just a formality and not the big glowing lamp at the end of it all.

The door clicks. The green light comes on in the cell-wall panel. It means the computer has unlocked all the cell doors. I don't move, just take in the sounds. What is out of place at this moment is the loud click-clack of a screw's footsteps. He's stopping at my door. He opens it and gives me a letter and a faintly token indication that he is pleased I am receiving a letter. The letter is out of the ordinary twice over. It's unusual to get any kind of letter at six in the evening and this has no stamp on the envelope. Nice one, it's from another friend in Holland. I read the first two paragraphs and stop. I hate rushing a letter, it's something to take slowly and stretch out like a bath. Besides it's the unwanted adrenalin that goes with an unexpected letter. Got to calm down, make the most of it and we're due out on exercise any minute. But I do know why the envelope has no stamp, it's come in a parcel. She's written at the start of the letter about sending me some things. I'll have to apply for them.

DOWNSTAIRS FOR OUTSIDE ASSOCIATION
DOWNSTAIRS FOR OUTSIDE ASSOCIATION

They really love that tannoy in Long Lartin and especially on cold mornings when I'm deep in my pit and what the hell is there to get up for. One joker of an SO, a well-spoken oddity on the receiving end of Joe's special attention, he used to make the call for breakfast sound all too wholesome like we were whistling cornflake kids. In his early days it was INMATES FOR BREAKFAST. Fucking inmates. Then, when punter enthusiasm was not what it should be, it was THIS IS DEFINITELY THE LAST CALL FOR BREAKFAST.

As it is now there's just a bland
LAST CALL FOR ASSOCIATION

This gets me up and I'm off down the corridors and out into the hot, still air. I'm due for a big run round the field tonight. The Harrier's got me at it. I salute my Irish mates standing round the wing wall they've made their handball court and decide I'll walk a lap or two before the run. Loosen up. I fall in a with a witty republican also in patches. We've gone no distance at all when I hear my name being called. Your man in patches points at arms waving through a window in the next bordering wing. The screw behind the arms calls my name again and I go down the slope to the window.

"Barker, there's these things in a parcel for you, you'll know about them."

"Yes sure, from Holland."

"That's right. If you sign for them here you can pick them

up from your own wing."

I put my hand in and as I'm signing the form ask casually what it is. The guard and his pal have smirks on their faces but they're embarrassed.

"Well Barker, there's some puzzles where you have to put a ball in a hole, a toy that goes Moo when you press it, and a toy mouse," he says. All this punctuated with laughs. The laughs are condescending and unnerved.

"Yes, right, of course," I say.

Back up the slope I tell your man the situation. He laughs. I analyze.

"Of course she is into crazy stunts. Maybe there's something inside it. No. Wouldn't stand a chance. When a toy mouse came down on the security desk you can bet they gave it a prodding."

Your man is no help, he's still laughing.

"Or maybe," I say, "she thinks this is an asylum. I've had my own doubts believe me and in Holland, you know what it's like, super-liberalism, the nasty sort where prisons and asylums are all the same thing, therapy all round."

Your man is not impressed with my reasoning. He does not aim to reassure. "Normally speaking," he says, "if I got a toy mouse off a woman I'd take it as a brush-off, an off-beat Dear John if you see what I mean."

"I do see what you mean but it's not that kind of situation, we're not close like that. Anyway why pick on the Johns, why not a Dear Gerry?"

We're coming back round to the handball wall and I'm going to have to get this run started. Maybe I'm taking it too seriously, this running, feeling tense like I am. Oh fuck it, I take off my pumps and put on the red headband I've made for myself in the workshop. The mouse goes out of my mind as I start to run, feeling the grass under my feet and between my toes. The grass isn't parched yet, no brillo pad feel, but the blades have begun to stiffen and they scrape and scrub luxuriously.

The pace is still easy and I can feel my lungs doing their work till the rhythm is there, legs and lungs pumping together. Nothing can go wrong. Turning the corner again, my face upwards, the sun is head on. The light sparkles through the sweat trickling in my eyes. For a while I could be anywhere, then finish with a three hundred yard sprint and collapse on the ground between the handball wall and the public park-type toilet, ready to spew up.

Your man spots me in this state and is over like a shot, ruthless bastard.

"It must be one of those clockwork mechanical ones, that mouse. They're going to have you down as a lunatic. Give it a few weeks and it'll be, Put me down for the Welfare guv, someone's nicked me mouse," he says in outrageous cockney.

"Yeah, yeah, yeah." It's all I can manage, I'm gasping.

"No, not the welfare, it'll be the psycho. Largactyl and sympathy. Officer, she'll say, the mouse and these games are essential to this man's sanity and rehabilitation."

"Look I can take one of two lines," I say, pressing on with the analytical tone. "Either I can make it whimsical, like how's about you take me off the A book, what self-respecting high-risk prisoner do you know with a toy mouse. Or I can just go in bold and front it out, Give me my mouse cunt."

The laundryman, another Irish wind-up merchant can't wait to get in his 5p's worth. He can't resist.

"Why not go in all dopey and daft and give it the old, Have you seen my mouse mister. Do it for the crack."

"Laundryman," I say gravely, "when they take you out for the firing squad and ask if you've any last words you'll say, But I only did it for the crack. And they're going to say, Oh yes Crack Crack. And you're dead, brown bread, full of holes."

The screws start moving in from the perimeter fence. The

dog-handlers look like their alsations, like they're ready to growl. Some cons move in ahead of time and get the bird, like they're sheep or what. In the corridor finally the Laundryman warms to his task. "Give them the full lash, have a tear rolling out of the corner of your eye, Go on give us me mouse guvnor."

"OK it sounds like a good stunt, sounds like it, but I haven't got the front to pull it off," I say. "Besides, supposing it backfires and they try to nut me off."

"That's pure paranoia."

"I've every right to be paranoid."

Back on the wing it's very quiet. I go straight to the wing office. Present is the slippery SO and two sidekicks. I've decided on my course, front it out. Only the atmosphere in the office is subdued, it does not suggest wisecracks at my expense.

"I believe you've a toy mouse of mine in here."

Slippery SO doesn't look up, he's well into a snowed-under-all-this-damn-paperwork routine.

"There's some things up on the cabinet for you," he says, and I can see he looks genuinely distracted. I grin wolfishly, that's how it feels, and pick up the parcel. I'm out quick and up on to the landing. It's quiet there too.

Joe comes into my cell.

"So, how was it in the office?"

"Nothing really, nothing happened, no wisecracks."

"See, all that paranoia, all that planning, making a big deal over nothing, that's your problem."

"A mountain out of a mousehole." Having taken a lot of stick in the last hour, I laugh loud at my own joke.

Joe winces, eyes the mouse and rams it under my nose. I can see a crazy blank look come over his eyes. I know this look, I'm wary.

"This is no mouse, this is a rat. A rat. A longtailed rat."

"Bollox, it's too small"

"Look at it's tail for fucks sake. Anyway I need to borrow it for a while."

"Hang about, I want a good look at if first."

He bends it a couple of times. Firm but flexible, just what the Governor would call himself. Joe dusts its whiskers and flicks its tail. He's looking dangerously vacant. I examine the rest of the parcel. There's a pink cylinder with holes in the top and a picture of some lobotomized cows stuck around it. I press it. Moo it goes, Moo. We laugh like crazy guys. The security screws must have had a wail of a time with it.

Phil comes in with an ear-to-ear grin. "You've heard the story then, the night's events."

"I'm not with you," I say as Joe makes those cows Moo and I stroke the mouse in my hand. Phil looks at it closely and the grin stretches some more.

"That's some rat," he says. "I could have done with it in my showdown with the human variety."

"It's not a rat, it's too small."

"Never mind the size, look at its tail."

They are stubborn these guys, I'm not getting anywhere so I change tack. "So what did go off tonight? They were distracted in the office just now, there was something else on their minds."

"You really haven't heard?"

"Heard what? We just got in off exercise."

"Wait till you've heard this, it'll put the dairy on your rat."

He can see me frowning.

"Rat, mouse, what's the odds because tonight saw a dramatic finale to the double agent's carer. You remember last week I told you he's got the message, that we knew he was a grass."

We could hardly have missed it, for a week Phil had been putting up regular cartoons showing the grass in action. They were a welcome change from all those Messages from the Governor and, taken all together, amounted to a Kama Sutra of grassing.

"Tonight it finally got to him," Phil said.

He sits down in the chair, me and Joe take seats on the bed and he gives us the full story. It seemed that the cartoons had taken their toll. The grass had been nipping out every morning to rip them down off the wing notice board. He knows Phil's behind it so he's given him a pull in the Weavers shop where they're both working. Phil's come straight out with it and tells him he's a known double-agent. He's been seen with a screw straight after some business has gone off in the workshop. The screws can't have seen anything of what went off but when the heavy mob arrive they know exactly who to go for. The grass really blows it then by saying he never talked to any screw which really got up Phil's nose, him denying it, because he's seen it with his own eyes.

So that's it, it's on the line. Obviously grasses are a menace. When you're doing a number that makes life a bit more human and fucks up the smooth running of repression at the same time, their existence means you've got to have eyes in the back of your head. We're not born that way so it's a strain. And it was getting worse. The parole system, which is early release at their discretion, had put grassing in full swing. What made these people even more dangerous is that they get to the point where they don't know what's real any more, they're sticking up names while convincing themselves one way or another that it's not really grassing. It gets worse still when they start coming up with names for things they know fuck-all about, they get so used to being centre-stage with some screw or the Governor that they don't like to let them down. We're all guilty of a bit of gossip and the seduction of being In The Know but the real difference between Phil and the grass is that Phil is a serious bloke. He does things that need a good head and plenty of arsehole so he doesn't talk about it much, let alone grass.

Anyway after their eye-to-eye in the workshop Phil's started to hear wide-eyed accounts of how this guy is a karate expert. Only the grass has had to strong it. How he's been attacked by seven heavies, not a decent one or two but seven, and how's he laid them all out. Spark out. But then everyone who says they're into karate, they're always a black belt at the least. Like ex-army screws, letting out little rumours about themselves. It's always the SAS or the Paras, never the kitchen or the fucking stores.

It turns out that while we'd been out on exercise Phil had been doing some cooking with Doug, a working pal from Birmingham and while they were eating the grass has come into Phil's cell and given him the same spiel. Seven geezers he's knocked out in a street in Brum. This scene doesn't happen anywhere but Brum's their home town and they know for sure it hasn't happened there. And then with a big pause stuck in the middle he's said, "I only give a man one warning, after that he's dead." The stuff Oscars are made of, Phil said. Him and Doug they've sat there like those characters you read about, Rubbing Their Eyes With Disbelief. It's not Doug's business but he thinks it could be the funniest thing since the screw that had his tea spiked with acid ripped off his uniform shirt and jacket to reveal a Mickey Mouse tee shirt and shouted at the PO to go fuck himself and his keys.

Next thing is the Sailor's come from the TV room to tell them that the grass is in there with his partner in villainy, none other than the soft-toy crank of my first ever exercise in the jail, and that he's told the whole room that he's going to sort those bastards out. Minutes later he's shot out the TV room giving it with arms, chopping movements. He's turned to the two duty screws out there, turned on his heels, thrown a stiff arm in their direction and told them the score. "Don't make a move or you're dead." The Sailor saw it all, the screws just sat there mouths opening and closing without a sound.

Which is more or less what Joe and I are doing, sat on the bed among the brown paper of my parcel. And what happens is the grass arrives at Phil's cell giving it all the karate sounds, the karate moves. Phil's not a heavy, not in the jail, but he's given him a dig and there's some wrestling on the floor by which time the TV room screws must have pulled themselves together and rung the bell because the heavy mob's arrived at the scene breathless, cons blocking the spur long enough for it to be all over by the time they're there.

"So what happened to the man himself?" I want to know.

"Fuck knows, back in his cell I guess. No one's nicked but the guards have got to know what happened."

"That explains it, no wonder they were subdued in the office, one of their top agents neutralized in action. Wish I'd been there to see the TV room screws."

"Oh yes, no question, the guards were the leading comics. Like fish in a fish tank the Sailor said."

While me and Phil are relishing the details, Joe's split with the mouse. It's not long and we hear a scream from the landing. Then another. Then a loud scraping and banging. We're just on our way out to see what's happening when Joe comes back in with a big grin, mouse in the hand, hanging by its tail. Phil's arms are spread out in mute question.

"Your man Jack," Joe says. "I waved it under his nose and you know gypsies, can't stand rats, can't abide them. So he's screamed and started whinging, You shouldn't have done that me son, it's not right. So I gave him another flash and this time he's roared and run into his cell. He's barricaded up with his bed."

"Outrageous, that is fucking outrageous. Even if it is a rat, which I don't accept for a moment, it's not supposed to be an offensive weapon. Someone's going to get the needle, it won't last the course."

Even as I'm speaking I know it's a waste of time, I'm locked up with dangerous nutters. Phil darts out and is quickly back. "All true," he says, "Jack's looking out of his spyhole pale as fuck and moaning to the Sailor."

So of course it's not long before I'm honoured by a visit from the Sailor himself.

"That's a dangerous weapon you've got there, " he says, "I think you should put it in my safe hands."

A rhetorical question seeing as he's already out the door with it. As a man we squeeze into my doorway for a good view. The Sailor's standing at Jack's door.

"Let me in," he says. "I've just checked it out, it's only a toy thing, nothing to worry about. I've given young Joe a pull, told him straight, he's a fucking tearaway."

"I'm not feeling too good," is all we can hear from Jack's cell.

The sailor carries on, the tone reassuring. "There's no point in banging yourself up like this. It might help to talk things over."

There's a scraping sound, Jack's door opens just a little. The Sailor eases himself in. We can just hear their voices. The Sailor's offering to make a cup of tea.

"Thanks lad, he just doesn't think that Joe."

"He's only a kid, that's how they are, you're right, they just don't think."

We creep out to get a good view. Jack's turning round get his snout and matches off the bed. There's a terrible scream, the Sailor's managed to slip it on his pillow. He runs out screaming, doesn't even see us. Phil nips in to recover the mouse with who knows what villainy in mind while the Sailor's away to tell all his pals what a coup he's had.

"Phil, please be careful."

I'm sounding pathetic myself, events out of my control.

"Someone's going to get so wound up they'll end up stomping on it."

"Don't worry about a thing."

"But I am worried."

"I just want to try it on Houdini."

OK, I feel better, Houdini he's a bit of a div, not likely to stomp on anything and fuck knows how he's got the name because Houdini wasn't a div except for all that death-defying stuff. I can see Phil from the doorway, he's gone up the corridor and placed the mouse on a gloomy bit of landing close to the man's cell. Moments later he's got Houdini out there and points in the direction of the mouse. My mouse. It's a dumbshow, we can't hear anything but we can read the body language. Houdini's got a dumb grin on his face and Phil, Phil must be persuasive because they've gone into the man's cell and come out with Houdini holding a brown paper bag. He looks at the mouse in the shadow and gets down on his hands and knees. Now he's waving the bag back and forth in its direction.

Phil's standing in the man's doorway giving us some kind of tic tac and the dumbshow's starting to make sense. He's persuaded Houdini to catch it in the bag. Yes, and I'll lay money he's got a piece of cheese in his other hand because it's one of those evenings. Joe and I creep down the passage for a better view. He has got a bit of cheese. Moves his arm slowly. What's the matter with him, can't he see the thing's not moving. Whatever Houdini's done on the out to wind up in here, whatever it was, he shouldn't have done it, never stood a chance. He brings down the bag. Folds the whole thing in his hand, looks closer. And is nearly angry. Poor sod. He shrugs.

END OF ASSOCIATION

END OF ASSOCIATION

I pick up the mouse and take it back to my cell then get a jug of water for bang-up. For the last minutes the landing is buzzing, cons moving about and exchanging magazines.

I'm in behind the cell door. It clicks as the computer locks us all in. I hear the screw's footsteps stopping and starting, looking in each spyhole. Now it's mine. The footsteps move off. I give the mouse a searching look. It's been well made, from the back, no question, it's very realistic. A sculpture comes to mind. I get a bit of stale bread from the table and smear it with marmalade, put it on the windowsill under the bottom bar. I stick it's head and whiskers in the marmalade so I can see it from the back. It looks like it's just climbed on the bread. Brilliant, much better as it is, a toy one. No noise, no mess, no feeding: no leaving it with someone like the budgie freaks do when they're dragged off down the block.

The next day on the way to work I hear the grass has made a less than half-hearted attempt to top himself. He's even left a note that says he doesn't bear any hard feelings against PHIL. The name written. Grassing from the grave, that would have been a new one. As it is, he'll have booked himself into a cushy jail. Later on I had to sign the property sheet again. There were three entries; at the bottom: ONE RUBBER RAT.

TIME TUNNELS

I REMEMBER THIS GUY in the Scrubs who had this thing about spaceships. Not the first, but he would catch you unawares and you'd hear from behind but unmistakably aimed at your ears:"I was reading this book which proves that spaceships landed on the earth thousands of years ago. There are these huge geometrical patterns in the sands of Mexico that have always been there. That's where the ships landed, there's no other explanation."

And I would curse Erik von Danikin the dodgy sounding guy who I'd got to know is behind all this. Another time it would be-"How else can you explain those marks in the rocks of Nova Scotia."

One time I'd just started to say something about natural erosion and just how much dough had Erik made out of all this when there's suddenly another dimension. This other guy who had a much wider taste for the outlandish; Arthurian legend, the Bermuda Triangle, Tolkien, and had now joined the spacemen as gods mob.

"You're desperately trying to write it off, " he said. "You're just imprisoned in logic. Some tribes in different parts of the American continent worship the same engraved stones which have the shape of a spaceship. These are tribes that can't have come into contact with each other yet these stones are the same. You're just so intolerant you people."

"I just can't stand mindless tolerance," I said, moving off at speed. He stayed in pursuit, shouting what was Moses' burning bush but an image of inter-galactic fuel.

Why am I remembering this now? It must be because my mate Joe has started to talk about L-L's corridors as time-tunnels. It's true, L-L is closer to science fiction with its flashing lights and electric locks; the Scrubs was more like a battered old submarine in a World War II movie with a crisis every five minutes.

"I was coming back through the time-tunnel from A Wing, it was packed with wanderers," he said.

"Condemned to wander for eternity," said Larry the pin-and-thread man.

"Eternity, that's fucking stronging it." Joe moves back and forth from brummie to cockney at will and the voice of a Dublin jackeen when he feels like it. "Sure they look like they're having a bad time, after all they've all just had the magic tot from the sick bay, but eternity, it's a bit much."

"Tell that to a lifer."

"Anyway I met Johnny Wax, number one LG down in the tunnel."

"LG?"

"London gangster, anyway you know what he said?"

Me and Larry do our best to look like a ring of blank faces.

"What are they like them new trainers you've got, that's what he said. That's all he saw, I was just the body went with the track shoes. He was worried in case he'd missed out on something, not having any."

"Yes, I can picture it," I said and the pin-and-thread man, who hates his collages being called pin and thread, nodded in agreement. "So what did you say, how are your sixteen quid track shoes?"

"I just said, Sorry Johnny, don't want to get caught in the time tunnel. He gave me a funny look."

"I bet he did. If he didn't rate himself so much he might have thought you were taking the piss. As it is, he'll have you down as a nutter," Larry said, his Black Country voice almost lively.

"And he may be fucking right at that," I said seriously. "I've had bitter experience of such cases."

"You calling me a case pal," Joe said in cockney hardnut mode.

"What cases," Larry said, stepping in.

"Cons who get hung up on spaceships, time tunnels, time capsules. Which is all down to the nick being isolated, insulated from the real world and with the particular nature of the fantasy depending on the physical characteristics of the jail." It sounded rehearsed as I spoke, I had a cartoon flash of myself as a psychologist with pince-nez who's got it all sewn up, but I'd thought about it too much to stop. "So the Scrubs for example, the wrought iron landings and stairways, that was submarine material."

"Boring," Joe said, "after a year you'd be saying, Not the fucking North Pole again."

"Sounds more like the Green to me," Larry said. "Only that's a tramp steamer, the oldest in the fleet, overdue for the knacker's yard."

"Well the Scrubs was definitely submarine, always gloomy with this polythene over the safety net."

"Safety net, that's rich. Fall on them and you'd be decorated for life, a ten of diamonds on legs."

I told the story of the paint bomb and how afterwards, it had been like living in a permanent winter's evening."

"Time frozen eh. This is one of those evenings when you try and sell an unwary con some theory or another," Larry said.

"Me, sell you a theory? Yesterday I couldn't sell you a biscuit I was giving away."

Joe stepped back into the fray, he was pissed off. "I don't think you appreciate just how close my escape from the time tunnel was."

"Stuff the time tunnel, that's just another spaceship number."

That's why I remembered the guy in the Scrubs, I cited him as an example.

"Wait a minute, you said submarines, in the Scrubs it would be submarines."

"Should have been, only Erik von Daneken had cornered the market."

BUT WHERE WERE WE, where did this remembering take place? We were in Larry's cell. Apart from the standard issue bed, table, chair and pisspot, it was furnished with a pile of Times crosswords in various states of completion; pin-and-thread boards, also in various states of completion; jugs of tea of vintages varying from half an hour previous to three days old. There also a record-player and many records including a Linguaphone   Teach-Yorself-Arabic course. International drug smuggling was a serious business he said. I was entirely ignorant of the language but his progress seemed slight. He did not deny it, said he got a sore throat after five minutes practice.

We were in the man's cell slowly eating a curry that had cost us most of what we called our wages. There was me, Joe, Houdini, the man of the house and Albert the Frenchman who was late. Then when we'd eaten our fill with some leftovers Gerry turned up. He was a black dude and experienced con who did well in Kalooki games with LGs. He had a mean temper but could be very funny and had introduced me to Nina Simone and Millie Jackson. As he came in he said he'd come in on a 4-1 winner at the start of the afternoon but still wound up fifty p down. It wasn't even as if Phil the bookie had done well, it was a novice punter who'd cleaned up on an outsider in the last race. He was scornful, said novices always went for something that was at least 20-1. His story moved us and he was invited in for something to eat.

"But if a man wants to do his bird as if it's a five year space trip," said our host, his eyes red from threading pins late into the night, "who are you to question it?"

"Fucks sake don't give me that sentimental chic, nutters are as sane as everyone else. The poor fuckers are all obsessive. We suffered enough from that bullshit in the sixties."

"And what bullshit is that wiseguy?"

"What? What? Just listen to this," I said. I was hopping, scrabbling through his records. He was methodical, this was a guy could tell you all the possibilities and permutations of flights from Tangier and Karachi airport, and the discs were arranged alphabetically. After "Weather Report" was "Live from Woodstock". I glanced across the disc and found what I wanted. It had started to rain and some bastard got the crowd to chant No Rain, No Rain as if that was going to stop it.

"See what I mean, it was a good scene, naive and commercial maybe but a bit subversive." I was shouting. "And what happens, bullshit, mystification. King fucking Canute."

Joe said yes, but he was sticking to the point even if I couldn't, obsessions that's where we'd been, and he'd come across it in the only good book he'd read about prison by some French geezer.

Naturally enough Albert wants to know who is this French geezer.

"Well he wasn't one of your Marseilles gangsters," Houdini said, though for all he knew he might well have been.

Albert was a Marseilles gangster, a sharp, sceptical romantic who'd come to London armed to the teeth so as he could rob something but got nicked down to getting mistaken for Carlos the Jackal. He also faced a life-sentence in France when his ten stretch was up. They said he'd offed a cop. I got the feeling he'd only die happy shooting it out with them. Meanwhile he was learning racy English fast.

"No, no," Joe said, flapping Houdini away. "This guy was called Victor Serge, he got done with the Bonnot gang way back and he's in the jail when the First World War broke out. The cons didn't even know it was on for a couple of years, didn't know anything was up till they heard the artillery close by and saw the screws doing a runner. Silence rules, no newspapers, how would they know."

"Huh, World War One, what is that to us."

"You don't go for the past eh."

"Huh, I shit on the past," Albert said, the sneer ferocious.

"What's all this got to do with spaceships," Houdini said.

"I bet you shit on spaceships too," Larry said before giving a cry of triumph at getting a nasty little four letter clue.

"Of course," Albert said. It made for a silence. I leapt in feet first. "Spaceships are the modern equivalent of this situation, insulation from the real world, only now it's self-made. I mean imagine us sitting here and all the while there's a world war going on which we don't know about."

"World Wars don't come in the same shape and size these days, anyway we've got TV," Larry said blandly.

"The TV," I shouted, "you think the Yanks or the Russians are going to wait for News at Ten to announce the fact before they get down to business."

Joe had been wearing a pained, martyred look for some time. "Very true," he said. "But if you've finished..."

The pause was epic.

"If you've finished I was going to say that Serge says obsessions are the main enemy in prison. He lists them, not just sex but cons going on about their cases. Hundreds of points the lawyers missed."

"Or pin-and-thread. There can't be anything more debilitating. Anyway, it makes you go blind."

Larry was nettled and he had a good memory. "First you said it was spaceships were the worst obsession, now you're saying it's collages."

"Ah, a point of logic. You can say that, Point of logic," Albert asked.

"Yes you can and I have got my just desserts for a cheap crack. You could put that one in the notebook Albert, just desserts," I said sounding magnanimous to my own ears.

"Or as the crossword clue said, comeuppance is only sweets we hear, " Larry said.

"You can't resist getting off the point you lot, can you," Joe said.

We were chastened. I was chastened. Unable-to-be-serious-for-long-periods, that could be added to the list of enemies in prison.

"So what's wrong with obsessions?"

"They take up too much time don't they, so much energy into something that won't get you anywhere."

"A bit like paranoia," Larry said thoughtfully. "All that energy into working out how to handle something that isn't going to happen anyway."

It was true. When it came on, heavy paranoia was like a roller-coaster poem, image slipping into image at breakneck speed. "In prison there's no reality to check these spirals," I said. "And because it all gets stale, experiences and sensations used over and over. It's why I've stopped taking acid in the jail. The sixth trip was the same as the fifth only boring with it."

The p-and-t man was in like a shot. "That's just because it's full of strychnine and speed these days. Can't get any decent acid."

Out of nowhere, out of a forgotten corner of the cell came an aggrieved voice, Gerry's. "Hey, there's no meat on this fucking bone."

We were rolling about with laughing. Anyone still eating afters coughed up rice pudding and cold tea, snorted it down noses, instant grits and sore throats. Into this noise stepped the clear inquiring voice of Albert. "Why exactly are you laughing?"

There was another wave of laughter. I struggled back into words. "Your ancestors would have been proud of you. Voltaire and all that, French anthropologists analysing the meaning of cannibal rituals from inside the cooking-pot."

Albert had many fine qualities, perseverance was one. "This is all very interesting but why exactly have you laughed when Gerry he has said that?"

"Well there we were getting all metaphysical," Joe said, "and Gerry's voice is bringing us down to earth, the nitty-gritty, the food."

"Ah English humour, it is always so, you do not like to fly very high. If you do, it is only so you can come down as quick as you can."

Joe looked narked, maybe it was being included in The English. "There you go, analyzing again," he said. "And come to that, why did you fucking laugh."

"Ah me, I have laughed because you offer him your curry, you offer it from the heart and he complains there is not enough, eh putain."

"Yes that's right, cheeky sod," I said

"All right then, when you've finished mauling the bones just look at this one. Go on, look, there's fuck all on it."

"Nowadays you're supposed to eat the bone dumbhead, they're edible plastic," Larry said.

"Lets get back to base for fucks sake," Joe said.

"Where is it sergeant?"

"Obsessions," I said, "their prevalence in prisons and the forms it takes, spaceships being one." To myself I sounded crisp and decisive.

"Magic."

I wanted to rip my hair out, had a flash of sympathy with those legions of schoolteachers that were supposed to be cracking up. "No, not magic," I screamed.

"Obsessions? What about screws, they're a prime example," Gerry said, finally, reluctantly finished with the curry. "With them it's all porn mags and overtime."

He was right. I remebered all the screws on detached duty who made up our trial escort. They'd talk about getting in eighty hours work as if it was an achievment.

"I'll tell you what," Gerry said, his voice serious. "In the fifties when they were still topping people they had a few screws on the death watch, four of them working in pairs, twelve hours on twelve hours off. They reckoned it was a real coup to get on it. I heard them talking about it years after, one screw bought a motor on the strength of it. That's the scales of justice."

"The cops are the same, wanting their whack out of honest criminals," Larry said.

"Fuck the cops, I don't want to talk about them again," Joe said.

"So which esoteric subject do you want to talk about then?" Larry said.

"There's no need to get a cob on," Joe said.

"Do you have one cigarette for me please," Albert asked.

There was a fumbling for tobacco and papers. Houdini had Rizla, that was it. And pay day only three days gone.

"That's how it is these days," Larry said. "Last week I had trouble poncing matches, fucking matches."

"What do you think it's like outside these days?"

"It may be bad but they sure as hell aren't poncing matches."

"Huh, now it is you English who analyze. I don't ask for this talking, I must have tabac."

"You could try that quiet geezer on the Ones, you know, Bob" Joe said with the helpful disinterest of a non-smoker.

"You know why he's quiet," I said, "because he doesn't want people rapping on his door all the time trying to ponce or borrow till Thursday. If he's got any sense he'll have a near empty poverty tin on display and the rest stashed away."

"That just shows what a mean and devious bastard you are."

"If I was a mean and devious bastard I'd keep a poverty tin and I'd have a smoke right now. I wouldn't have this problem."

"If you've a problem go and see the Welfare," Joe said.

It was a cheap crack, Albert wasn't standing for any more, he was clambering out over knees and legs.

"Please, I must search one for tabac."

"It can't be that desperate, you're not going to give someone a rub-down," Houdini said.

"Huh, you are so stupid. I have money. I find someone with tabac and we deal."

I admired Albert's confidence and clarity and remembered our expertise in the Scrubs. It seemed like every night we had half an ounce between us and cut it five or six ways without argument.

"There's no doubt about it, I've noticed a real shortage in the jail recently," Larry said. "It must be we're short on wages. Must be, I'm going on Governor's about it."

"On Governor's," Joe said. He was amazed. "You must be mental. What do you want, sympathy?"

"No, I've got an unanswerable argument."

"Jesus, Mary and Joseph," Joe said with a quick shift to Dublin. "You're all the same you liberals and hippies. You think you'll get things just because you've got a good argument, as if deep down everything was fair but for a few slip-ups, that you can win things just because you're reasonable. If it was like that, half the world wouldn't be starving."

"All right then, I'll suggest we could have fags in free like some jails in the States, or at least they could take the tax off for prisoners."

Gerry was prepared to meet him on his own ground. "If they did that they'd lose the tax on our tobacco, they'd lose out."

Larry sprang to his feet. It was unprecedented. He was glowering with scorn. "What they'd lose from that wouldn't pay for a lollipop lady at a zebra."

"The point is they don't want to make things easy for you, it's punishment. If you want anything you're going to have to fight for it, have a strike, then give your arguments. Anyway you can bet with spending cuts and that, the Home Secretary isn't going to be pleading with the Treasury to improve the wages of poor cons."

I came in sounding suspiciously like the other half of a double act. "It's all down to power and the only real power we have is to make them nervous about the whole place going up."

"All power corrupts," Larry said.

"What? What the fucks that got to do with anything? Anyway the people who say that are the people who've already got plenty of it. If it's all corrupt why bother to change things, which just happens to suit them down to the ground."

I jumped in again, the double act seamless. "Fucking right, it's all that original sin bollox, human nature is corrupt. Even if it was true then you have to organize power so that not just a few people have it. What really corrupts is powerlesness."

"And the nick is a perfect example," Joe said, "having no power corrupts us into cynicism or childishness. And to put off seeing what a disaster it is and how powerless we are, bosh, the retreat into fantasies and obsessions."

"So you want a grey, uniform world where fantasies are not allowed eh, Joe Stalin."

Joe sighed. Then he said, "Have your fantasies but they're a fuck sight better if you make them real."

The cell door pushed open and Albert came in dead-pan. The legs between him and his chair gave way like the sea for Moses. He was a respected man saying nothing. He dragged it out. He sat down. The half ounce of Old H appeared in his hand with a flourish. It was still wrapped in its cellophane and made that crinkling sound we knew so well.

"Yes, I had always believed Charlie to have some tabac and behold, I have conquered," Albert said, pleased as punch.

Tobacco was broken up, teased out between finger and thumb, laid out along Rizlas and rolled. A beautiful fragrance filled the cell.

"Now talking about fantasies and obsessions," Gerry said, content with the first down-to-the-diaphragm tote on his roll-up, "put the two together and you get your con who's gone religious."

"They're just parole-punters."

"No, with some of them it may start off for the jam-roll but they end up believing it, I've seen it happen."

"God's like the Home Office," I said, "the power above that's always out of reach."

"I'll tell you what though," Gerry said, "that Vicar does love a face. I mean fuck the poor and meek, he's choosey."

"That's true now you come to mention it," Larry said, "you get the nonces going in numbers but he don't give them any time."

Joe was busy in the cold, left-over rice, head down, doing some purposeful eating. Everyone else was waiting for someone else to declare their thirst first and that this same someone else would go and make some tea with the last of the tea-bags.

It was Larry cracked first, suggesting someone go down to the boiler and do it.

"You do it since you obviously want it the most."

"I did some of the cooking."

"What's that got to do with it, you dealers are all the same. Here and now it's you wants the tea, so you should go and make it."

"Are you saying you don't want any Gerry? Anyway I was only making a suggestion, nothing more."

"Fucks sake either do it or don't do it but lets not lose track again," Joe said.

"So where were we?" Houdini said.

"Obsessions as a cause and sign of powerlesness, " I said, trying hard to be precise.

"You sound like the Prosecutor in my trial as it happens," Gerry said.

"Obviously one of the best then, razor-sharp was he?"

"Well I'm here, don't know if that means anything to you boys," Gerry said, like he was a white gent of the southern USA."

"Now these places, they let you know about powerlesness pretty quick," I said. "You remember those browns you get on remand, Jesus they were terrible."

"A terrible experience for you John, very traumatic."

"It was as it happens but then there were some great moments even wearing that shit. Like my first trip in Brixton. I went out on exercise and it started to snow. I was walking round with my face in the air, the snowdrops hitting me on the face. They were huge, breaking on impact into hundreds of cascading crystals."

"They're great those moments," Joe said like he was suddenly far, far away. "It slaughters the screws. They can take all that grin-and-bear it stuff and they don't mind if you crack up as long you don't start carving them up, but to have your own cheerfulness that they can't steal off you, it does them up."

"Wait a minute," Gerry said, "you were the one going on about escape into fantasy, what about acid, how was it the next day without your little helper."

"I've already said, I've packed up using it in here but as it happens, well when I came in off that exercise I must have had a big grin because the geezer who'd flogged me two of them, microdots they must have been, he wants to buy one back, only I can't find it, must have dropped it, so there he is crawling about on the floor for it, and I suddenly realize we're the only two not banged up and I'm off my nut but just waiting for the screw to arrive and ask what the fuck we're up to. And all the geezer can do is whinge. Anyway I've never said that acid is the ultimate reality."

"Now you sound like my defence brief," Gerry said.

"How was he?"

"Unconvincing obviously."

There was a long silence. Larry picked up one of his crosswords. Albert suggested a game of chess. No takers. Instead Larry came out of his crossword, something had been on his mind.

"But do the screws really care. Do they actually care about whether you're cheerful or not cheerful. It's a warehouse to them, nothing more and half the ones here are ex-car workers, they don't give a fuck as long as the pay cheque's coming in."

"What you say, have you not read of those prisoner records they found in that riot. Huh, fucking screw, they call me Albert like I am their friend but in their reports they will write Albert is schizophrenic, is psychopath, that is screw for you."

"But a screw like Roundface isn't reading Teach Yourself Psychology in his spare time, he sticks to the porn."

"What got me was one report said, This man is mixing with the wrong people. You'd have thought we were all the wrong people by definition."

"Ah, a point of logic," Albert said.

"And if you try and play it safe by mixing with no one they call you anti-social like the Harrier."

"So that's their power," Joe said. "If they want they've got you fucked whatever way. Another record they found in the riot was of this toerag who scabbed on a strike there and what does it say, This man did not join the strike because he hopes to wheedle parole in this way."

"At least that sounds true."

"The point is that if you're in a situation where you can't win, that's got to be an absolute defeat," Joe said. "That's the power of the ruling class. The power to control what prizes you can or cannot win. So here you can win a few things within the limits but they're not worth a carrot anyway."

We were on new ground, but somehow things I'd been thinking about after bang-up, week after week, seemed to be making a picture.

"Of course it's a defeat to be in here, " I said. "But it doesn't have to be a total defeat. Isn't that what we've been talking about. And one way not to be defeated is not to start thinking this is the whole world or retreat into fantasy."

"Narrowing your horizons with a vengeance."

"You can say that, narrowing your horizons. Is very English. You have horizons so that you can narrow them."

"Look I'm going to make some tea seeing as no bugger-else will," Larry said, "but before I go I'm going to say this: I can't see as how screws are so busy fucking us up like by making us think this is the whole world."

"It's their whole world that's for sure," I said. "but it doesn't matter what they think or what their motivations are, they're just operating the routine. Like I remember this AG telling me we had to relate as human beings and him getting the right hump when I said I didn't give a monkeys whether he as an individual was good, bad, or indifferent."

"So you insulted his ego. Big deal," Larry said, levering himself out of his corner spot and cautiously lowering his feet to the ground. What a meal he made of it, like he was stepping into a blizzard.

"I may be gone some time," he said, like he really did believe it.

"Don't die in the snow martyr."

"When you get the tea find out what the time is."

"What do you want, jam on it," he said, his passing shot as he pulled open the door and let in a wall of muted wing noise.

"That's what screws want, jam on it," Gerry said. "They want to lock you up, fuck you up, and then they get the needle if you don't like them."

"Like colonialists," Joe said quietly.

From a long silence on his part Houdini came to life and said we were all on the wrong track. We were in prison, it was no good, we wanted out and never mind horizons or the rest.

"I saw this prisoner in a TV documentary," he said, "and he hit it on the nail."

"What did he say?"

"They call me institutionalized, he said, but they won't take me to the main gate and open it to see which way I'd go."

"Fair point," Gerry said. "Still there's comfort, security, three meals a day, central heating, laundry, no bills, what more do you want."

"Yes, and if you hear a police siren like you could in the Scrubs, you knew it wasn't for you."

"And good company," Houdini said, carving himself an empire from our host's vacant corner.

"Yes but what about those times in a local or somewhere there's no Night Sanitation and you're banged up for the night, you slowly roll a fag, reach down to light it and there's no fucking matches. You search the same places over and over because you just can't believe it, what then?"

"Severe gnashing of teeth."

Larry came in clutching a jug of tea. He saw immediately that Houdini had taken his favourite spot but said nothing. Albert meanwhile had got pissed-off with our flippant five minutes. "Evidently you like it here. You have just provided a list of amenities but they are nothing compared to your freedom."

"The gilded cage no good for you eh Albert."

"Ah you English", he said and Joe winced so we could all see him wincing. "You English laugh it away. I admit I like the heating, without it I'd die in this fucking English weather, but all this TV, and now with colour, it is nothing to your freedom."

As he spoke Albert came out of his chair in a fighter's crouch. The rest of us were caught up in a sequence of moving legs, horizontal choreography, Gerry's legs swung up, my legs swung up like we were ripples and Larry the stone as he slowly regained his spot with a wedge movement on the bed. Houdini didn't have a chance, Larry was very experienced at this game.

When the ballet'd eased off he told us it was half eight, then Joe weighed in again.

"I go along with Albert. What's the odds having this or that. OK this nick is better than a local but so what, all you can say is it's not all bang-up and piss-pots."

"And rats," Larry said, pausing for effect.

He was successful, we were all ears.

"When I was in the Green," he said, expansive from his re-secured base, "this bloke tells me he's woken up in the middle of the night and there's something crawling over him. So he lights a match and sees it's a fucking rat. So he goes sick in the morning and tells the doc. You know what he did, what he prescribed? A cat for the night."

"A lucky man," I said. "Number one he had a match. Number two he's struck lucky with a pragmatic doctor. Any other and it would have been largactyl for delusions. Or said it was a false and malicious allegation, dished out more largactyl, ghost-trained him and then hijacked some remission."

"OK, OK, locals are worse, I don't deny it," Joe said. "But in locals they're not doing Tens and Fifteens. That's what prison is, you only know what it is when you've done a few stretch and there's more to come."

"Sure, and in return I've known guys get obsessive about one jail or another, I've still got hankerings for the Scrubs. But you take women's prisons for example. Long term prisoners in Holloway are doing their bird in conditions of a short-term local more or less. Are you going to tell them it makes no difference?"

Silence.

More silence.

"The main thing is not to be in prison at all," Joe said finally.

"A defeat, of course," Albert said. "To be here at all, we are the mugs. Me, I have no luck at all, but still I am the mug."

The concentration in the cell was tangible. This was serious stuff.

"Yes, it's a defeat," I said, my voice qualifying that from the off.

"But?" Joe said knowingly, like I was Home Secretary Merlyn Rees or some other tricky but predictable bastard. But I was committed now, I ploughed on.

"But it's not a total defeat full stop. Consciously or not we do start to make our own space here. I'm not saying freedom, but even in this place that's custom-built for control, we make our own spaces that they never even thought of in their blueprints. "

"Huh, that is not freedom, that is survival only," Albert said.

"Making the best of it, exactly," Joe said. "But it's the best of something that isn't worth having. You're talking like some reformist when you know the reforms aren't worth a carrot. What difference does it make if the reforms are made by you or them."

"What are you talking about you jackeen's bollox," I said using his standard line of abuse. "I'm not talking about reforms and as it happens it's always us that makes them, they never give anything unless they have to. And as it further happens there's no way I'm saying you should forget you're inside. You ever seen curtains in my cell, ever seen me try and hide the bars. What I'm saying is you've got to live out the contradictions. You've got to make some kind of life here cos you're not dead, but never forget you're in the jail and that it's totally abnormal and anti-life."

"You're just playing their game."

"Look man, like Gramsci said, we're always playing someone's game, what's important is to play your own game and win."

"When it comes down to it, you can't win in jail."

"Who is this Gramsci man?" Albert asked.

"An Italian communist in jail under Mussolini, died inside after doing ten stretch."

"Not much of an advert," Joe said. "The fact is that sooner or later you always come up against the bars. Escape is the only priority."

"Yes, that is exactly so," Albert said.

"OK, it's a priority," I said. "These post-Mountbatten security jails are getting an aura of invincibilty that could do with getting punctured, but you've got to want to do it. No good saying it should be a priority for everyone."

Since the arrival of the Old H the cell had got a fug. Outside there was an outbreak of wing noise. Either the TV film had finished or it was close to bang-up.

"The fact is if you do not seriously wish to escape it is the end, n'est ce pas. You are cabbage already."

"But I've only two stretch left, it's not worth my while."

"And you have never tried?"

"Yes, once, 1974, out of the Scrubs but I got shanghaied here just when we were ready."

"An informer?"

"Don't think so, not for that. Anyway I think I had illusions, that the system was cracking up but then Labour kept the show on the road, swamped everything in their usual treacle."

"Huh, it is enough for me that I want to be free, it is nothing to me what is happening outside. Bah, politics."

"And I'm a prisoner of war," Joe said, "any time is the right time for me."

"And you make progress?" Albert asked.

"No comment."

"If I wanted to go, I'd just pal up with Dave Martin, he's got to succeed one time."

"Hey, it's ten to nine," Gerry said.

Larry sprang to life as he did every night. There was no tea left, who was going to get some tea. "I've got some sugar if you can get milk and tea."

"I've got the milk," I said, "but I'm not going on the ponce again. Since I've known you I've suffered a severe loss of credibility and my credit rating's down."

"The two of you, you're the nearest thing to a swarm of locusts."

"That doesn't get us nearer the tea," Larry said, diving out the door.

ASSOCIATION ENDS

END OF ASSOCIATION

"Now this is the time you really know you're not free. You're talking, feeling good, but it ends not when it's ready to end but when that that fucking tannoy starts."

"Exactly, you've come right round to what I was saying," Joe said.

"Bollox, I never disagreed about that."

LABOUR

THE TEXTILES SHOP was a joke, a Noddy shop. It contained forty sewing machines in three rows and had weak lights. The tannoy played the radio, Tony Blackburn and David Hamilton strong and mushy all day unless there was racing in the afternoon. There were three instructors led by cue-ball, two discipline screws and a civvie. If a machine broke down they'd stand around looking at it till the con mechanic could fix it. I worked as a packer with Alex. He said all you needed for an instructor's job was a white coat and a worried look. I'd started the job early on in a run of Wendy Houses. Alex said I was lucky to have missed the previous run of space suits. "Silver paint coming off in your hands all day long. But then look at this rubbish," he said, pointing to a pile of Wendy Houses. "Tell me seriously, would you buy a kid one of these on the out."

"No, but someone must do."

"Imagine them in a gust of wind. There's dad watching proudly when, Fuck me darling, nipper's roof's blown off."

"You know we're supposed to double up as quality controllers," he said a couple of days later.

"Sure, that's why we fill in these form sheets and reject two per day."

"Yes, well cue-ball must have sussed it, always two per day, said he hoped we realised we were supposed to be checking them."

"What, rejecting other cons' work, that's a bit much."

"It's a fucking joke anyway, the material's about as thick as this Rizla," Alex said taking one out of his tin and rolling up. "Cue-ball said the company had returned a batch."

"Who's the company?"

"Fuck knows. Snide and Snide? I could see he was extra worried, he's blotted his copybook, but what do they expect?"

We took our tea-break by the hot water urn. Scots George off the wing was already there. I'd got to know him better; how he only rated a piece of hash if it made him real paranoid, wee beasties coming out of the wall; how he'd rearrange the cell furniture if he got depressed. Sometimes he'd shade the cell light green and it'd be like he was in a fish-tank. On this morning he was talking about Scottish polecats.

"You see one of those and you make a very fast bodyswerve, " he said, indicating a polecat some six feet in height.

"And what, it chased you all over the highlands and lowlands," Alex said.

"That's right, I'm no joking."

"Fuck off George, you've never been out of Glasgow, what was it down for a day trip from the Highlands, down for the Sales?"

"OK don't believe me, just because you limey's have got nothing wilder than a hedgehog."

"Aye aye, burglars, are you sweet John." Alex said as two screws moved towards us.

They had come for me and as it happened I had no contraband of any sort. It made the cell-spin a relaxed affair for me. Only on the wing, outside my cell door before they did the business, the red-faced military looking screw asked me if I had anything to declare, like he was in Customs.

"What?"

"Is there anything you want to tell me about before we commence the search," he said with a tough glare.

It was hard to credit, what did he take me for. The search took an hour and a quarter. I was back in the shop for the last ten minutes of labour and told Alex the pre-search patter.

"Oh him, that's superscrew, he's supposed to have been a screw in New Zealand, Australia and South Africa."

"What's he want, a bonus for international experience."

I could picture the bastard in South Africa and wondered what villainy he'd got up to in the jails there.

I checked out my wages at the end of the week. As a packer I was on related earnings, they depended on how fast the machinists had worked. I found out from the con clerk that I'd lost out on the cell-spin. The rate for such time was half a pence an hour. I pulled the civvie who ran the shop. He was a local who'd had some small slice of the contract for building the jail and had managed to hang on in for this number. A miserable sod, free every evening, free every weekend and still he was miserable. I said it was out of order for me to be penalized for a cell spin I didn't want, had definitely not asked for.

"You'll have to see the Governor about that. Those rates come direct from the Home Office. They set them."

"You're having a laugh, what's he going to do, give me a

petition? I'll have finished my bird by the time I get an answer."

He gave me a miserable scowl and said there was nothing he could do.

Soon after the clerk got a transfer. I could genuinely claim job experience. I got an office with the job, partitioned off in hardboard and glass looking straight across at the Instructors' office. There was more work to the job than there'd been in the Scrubs. PRINDUS had made a complicated wage structure built on the piece-rates they imposed. Machinists would get a sticky tag for each completed box of five Wendy Houses which I had to stick on their wage sheets. In addition to the cell-spin rate there was a machine breakdown rate of one pence per hour. A week of that kind of money wouldn't go far. It was to deter sabotage but had not considered the antiquity of the machines. On top of all this there was a three-tiered structure of related-wages. Top rate for the mechanic, lower for me and the packers, and bottom rate for the trimmers. It was a toytown version of some big company, the picture completed by a mini-conveyor belt that never worked.

Like most everyone else, to escape the work routine I'd sometimes go sick to try and get a day's Rest In Cell. On sick parade there's be anything from 10 to 40 cons. After a while the doctor would sweep in followed by a white-coated SO who was the real decision-maker in the whole lottery. A white-coated screw would take up his place behind a half-door to dispense the different coloured medicines you might get lumbered with as the price of a day off. When your time came the doctor would ask what was the matter without looking up.

"It's my stomach, it's burning and I feel sick."

"Milk of Magnesia. Next."

This was the moment to make a stand.

"I'm feeling weak, I need a day's rest."

The doctor would look up for the first time. He was always

in a hurry. I'd heard he was a golfer and owned a glider. A busy man. He'd once dealt with 28 cons in 7 minutes. Meanwhile the SO would deftly produce your record sheet and whisper in the doctor's ear. That was it, you got it or you didn't. If you scored you'd be locked in for the morning and then again for the afternoon. If you wanted, there was a way around it, use the squawk box in the wall to get hold of a screw in Control Centre, say you needed a shit, then keep out of the way in a Cleaner's cell. If a wing screw got on your case you could have a shit; the screw could hardly say, Can't you shit faster. They were not that cheeky and it embarrassed them, our semi-public shitting.

There were times when a change was as good as a rest and the chokey was the place. In L-L it was the place, in Wandsworth or Dartmoor, a different story. I was down there on and off in support of Republican friends when they were fucked about. The quickest and simplest way which didn't log up that much lost remission was to refuse labour. You'd get locked in your own cell till they got an escort together for that walk along the corridors to the chokey, the Segregation Unit.

Several times I wound up down there as part of a protracted personal battle over the cell light. It was housed in a clouded glass casing. I kept unscrewing it, taking it off to get some half-decent light. Sometimes I'd screw it back on before falling asleep, other times I was incapable, forgot, or was too pissed off, and there'd be warnings and nickings.

The jail's own hearings were called Adjudications and took place in the chokey office in the morning. Two screws marched me in and stood close together between me and the Governor. The chief officer and the screw who'd nicked me were also there. The Governor asked If I plead Guilty or Not Guilty. This time I said I wouldn't plead.

"Very well, I'll enter that as a plea of Not Guilty," the Governor said. "Officer Clarke will give his evidence and then you have the right to ask questions through me."

In Plod language the screw said that removing the light-casing constituted a fire-risk and that I'd bee warned about this several times. The Governor wrote it all out in long-hand. It was a slow business. The screws facing had their heads lowered. They folded and unfolded their arms, stifled yawns. Sometimes they'd look up at nothing before lowering their heads again.

"You've heard Officer Clarke's evidence Barker, do you have any questions?"

"Did he know that I'd already registered a complaint on the Wing about the effect on my eyesight?"

"I can answer that," the Governor said. "Whatever you said on the wing is not relevant here. You have tampered with prison property and created a fire risk."

"So why are the cell lights designed so that in order to get a decent reading light there's a fire risk."

"You seem to think you're a special case. Other inmates seem to manage. I'm not having inmates with special privileges in this prison. Any questions."

I shook my head and there was a long silence while the Governor looked at his notes as if there were now a separate process of weighing the evidence and reaching his verdict. Sometimes I'd been taken out during this time. This time he looked and up and said, "I find you Guilty as charged. You will forfeit seven days remission to be suspended for Twentyeight days."

I'd lost wages before, lost remission, but this was new, suspended, a fucking bender like they really were a court of law. Over the next few weeks I made more of an effort to screw the cover back on before sleep.

Apart from these odd breaks I was working a five day week. I felt good on Friday afternoons and sometimes good on Thursdays if I'd got away with topping up the wage sheets.

It would involve stubborn argument with the boss who would spend hours going over the totals I'd come up with. In his miserable Worcester voice he'd contest every penny, every halfpenny. A one-man mission to curb Public Expenditure and it wasn't even his fucking money.

Sometimes the crack was good, sometimes I was bored stiff. David had a spell there and we had a good time. Then he was moved to the Engineers shop just as it won a contract to produce prison beds for Saudi Arabia, a serious contract with penalty clauses for late delivery.

"Twentyfive thousand prison beds?" I asked. "Are they expecting a crime-wave. Anyway I thought they just cut your hands off."

"Must be changing, must have decided jails are an essential part of being civilized," he said.

Soon afterwards we began a new contract for prison pillow cases. Compared to the Engineers, the Textiles was a noddy shop but this didn't stop PRINDUS increasing the intensity of labour with this new contract, imposing a speed-up. To get top wages they wanted over a hundred a day which was much harder then the Wendy House quota.

Maybe they thought that as they were pillow cases on which cons would lay their heads, the job should take that much less labour time. Maybe there was a Civil Servant who thought his posting to PRINDUS the equivalent of a diplomat sent to Mali, but who had resolved out of spite or wishful thinking to make something of it, to make it more profitable within its own terms. I had thought about what those terms were. They must have excluded the cost of reproducing the convict, his board and keep, most of which went in screw wages. I wondered if Tolworth Towers had some sophisticated accounting system which allowed for some of this cost and, in the case of pillow cases, that the Prison Department was both producer and buyer.

Whatever the reason, it suited the Prison Department's permanent interest in discipline. There's a clear relation between profitability and discipline, and the Department was interested in both. They had built HMP Coldingley as a copy of a big factory with a longer working day and a whole regime geared to the workshops with bonuses and fuck knows what else. Were selective about who was sent there, short-termers and lifers who were being considered for release. They were dead fussy too, a couple of steps out of line and the Lifer would be out on his ear, back in a long-term nick with his EDR slipping a couple of years into the future. It was nearly all unskilled manual work, as if they wanted cons to feel at home doing the kind of work they'd become criminals to avoid.

On the second day of the new contract the Sailor, having a spell as a machinist, gave cue-ball a pull. Cue-ball said it was a time-and-motion decision and there was nothing he could do about it. I remembered this neat, long-haired creep with an attache case. He'd been in the shop a couple of weeks back to look at the pillow-case material. George had said he looked that much like a fish he was entitled to jump in the fish-tank that livened up the instructors office. He had to have been the time-and-motion man. In the afternoon tea-break a strike was discussed. The new rate was going to mean a wage-cut, there was no two ways about it; only Griffiths, a greyhound of the sewing machine, was going to be able to meet the quota; it was a liberty; it was downright snide. The Sailor was for a strike.

"How about we try it first, go as fast as we can for half an hour and see how it goes," Pete said.

"I'll go along with that," said another.

"What's the sense in that," the Sailor said, "I couldn't even get top whack on those tents."

"No, be fair, if we show it can't be done, they haven't got a leg to stand on."

"They havna a leg to stand on anyway."

"What you done then George, kneecapped them?" London Tony said.

George gave him a look till the laughter died down.

"What you talking about you bam, I just tickled his hamstrings with my chiv," he said.

"Lets agree on something for fucks sake otherwise we'll be here rabbiting all day."

"Lets do this experiment now then, get it done with," said Dave the Hells Angel.

"Well if that's what you want," the Sailor said. "You suggested it Pete, do it with Norm, he's about norm for the speed."

A stack of blue boxes full of ready-cut material were dragged to their machines which were next to each other.

"Half an hour's worth, a ten thousand metres race. We don't want these boys getting sore fingers for nothing," the Sailor said.

A sidelined dopedealer did some mental maths. In reality we worked a six-and-a-half hour day. We were looking at eight in half an hour, your man said. George ran a small book in the shop with Alex. He promptly opened one.

"I'm putting my money where my mouth is, evens on Pete, Five to Four against Norm."

Tempting odds. I fancied Pete at evens.

"Come on you bams, Five to Four's more than fair, where are the sportsmen?"

He took two bets on each of the runners.

"Come on, I'm risking my all and I'm taking bets till the halfway stage, five furlongs, five thousand metres, whatever you like. I'm only saying the odds might well shorted with two such thoroughbreds."

"You're fucking mad," Alex said in a loud whisper, "it was Pete suggested it, he'll be going flat out."

"You havna studied the form man, " George said quietly. He was a shit-hot machinist. If he weren't the best maker of a pair of strides, if he weren't so busy with this bootleg business, he would have matched Griffiths in official production. Now he shouted, "Show some faith in the lads."

He got another two punters, then made a big deal out of the second hand of his watch coming round to bang on Three o'clock. "And they're off."

Norman promptly got his first pillow case in a tangle and a big cheer from everyone bar his backers. George said he was a novice put off by the starting stalls. "But he's a trier, got a good finish."

Pete got off to a flying start, three done in ten minutes, ahead of schedule. George stayed cool and took another two punters. I was reaching for my last fifty pence, only the Sailor said I was a mug.

"You watch him tire, he needs Lester on board to time his run in."

"Pure shite," George shouted back. "He's running well within himself. Feel the cloth man, a bit on the soft side, just how he likes it."

The crowd leaned in on Pete.

"Come on my son, you can do it," a punter shouted right in his earhole. Pete gave a start and the thread got tangled. He tried to steam on through the mess and the thread broke. There was the usual farting about re-threading.

"Christ sake don't lick it, cut it," Griffiths shouted.

"Give him space there, don't crowd him."

"More haste less speed," a con who'd made no bet said.

Why don't you go fuck yourself," shouted back a Five to Four taker.

Norman had relaxed but Pete was strained, the broken thread had got to him.

"You've been fucking nobbled," a backer shouted.

On the half hour the News came on the radio. The value of the pound had fallen, it was due to a strike at British Leyland.

George was magnanimous. The two runners were both on the seventh pillow case. There were machinists and machinists he said to Alex. "Give them a hand lads," he shouted out. "They gave their all, look at the sweat."

It was true, sweat dripping. They were paraded in the Instructors' office.

"Look at them, they've worked their balls off and that was only half an hour. It can't be done."

"It's a Home Office decision," Misery said.

"So just ring them up and say it can't be done," the Sailor said.

"It's not as easy as that. You can't change things just because you don't like them. Just give it a go. I'll guarantee you never have to wait for cloth."

"But we've just tried it, a you deaf or something. It just can't be done."

By then it was the end of the working day. The discipline screws opened the gates, ticked us off and rubbed us down. The sun was shining warm, a wind-up, going straight back into the septic corridors with their own dull light and air.

The next day few machinists worked though a strike had not been called as such. Two sex-cases worked along with a Manchester guy who was supposed to be sound and said to be a heavy, him and his pal. I wanted to give him a pull. Alex said I was crazy. "What can you do about it. We know he's a no-good slag and that's it, we know."

The general stoppage became a strike proper when the instructors went round the shop asking if cons were refusing to work. This was not the same as refusing labour, we were all at work, but it was a declaration. Soon after the jail's Chief Officer arrived. He was a smiler, a relic from the future wherein, it is wrongly assumed, prisons amongst other things would become progressively more liberal. It looked as though there might be a break in the case and a crowd formed round him.

"Well lads even though you're technically disobeying an order by not working…"

"No one's ordered us to work," Dave said.

The discipline screws moved in to back the Smiler. He kept on smiling.

"Be that as it may," he said, "you are technically breaking prison rules. But this needn't get in the way, it's obvious there's been a breakdown in communication."

"It's simple, we've been given a rate for a new job that's impossible to do. We know, we've tried it," the Sailor said.

The Smiler smiled some more. "I don't have the authority to do anything about that here and now but I can tell you the right way to go about it and this isn't it."

George was outraged. "It's simple, just ring up the Home Office, tell them the rate's impossible and that they won't get any production till they lower the rate."

"What are you going to come up with if we do return to work?" Norman asked.

"What I can do is talk to your instructors and see if some communication can be established whereby what you are saying can be taken into account. But I can say now in all sincerity that your action is not making things any easier."

After he'd gone there were suggestions that we go back to work and see what happened after a couple of days. I'd said nothing right through, I was only the clerk, but this had to be bollox.

"Why do you think the Chief's come in at all. Why's he even talking about how things might be changed. If we just complained and went on working they wouldn't give a monkeys."

"Hang on, you're not even on a machine."

"He's on related pay, we get nothing, he gets nothing," the Sailor said. "And lets have it right, we stay out till we get what we want."

The next day cue-ball announced they were in communication with the Home Office but that we should go on working.

"He's just trying it on," Alex said. "They were looking to see if they could get away with it and they'd wear it. Give it another day and it won't be worth the aggravation to them."

The Manchester head didn't get a pull from anyone but he was getting the blank and his work slowed to a crawl. Next day he didn't show at all, the slippery bastard had got a labour transfer in double-quick time. So me and Alex had a good laugh in the afternoon when cue-ball announced the rate no longer applied. He dressed it all up and went on about averages which hadn't taken something into account, and how it would all have come to light anyway. For a while after that it was a good crack in the shop.

Manoeuvres

IT WAS EERIE but somehow insulting to be sat in the TV room of Long Lartin watching cons on the rooftop of Hull prison. 'The revolution will not be televised,', feeling that's how it ought to be. The midday news featured at least one friend behind a mask. The fact I was able to watch it all seemed to say something about the insufferable self-confidence of the prison system. But then as far as the riot went, the main concern of the Home Office was to be seen to be in control, not panicking. To have disarmed the TVs of other max-security jails would have been a sign of weakness and as likely as not, set them off too.

The cons looked great with their balaclavas, blankets and banners high up on the rooves. Prisoner Officers had evacuated the cell-blocks but maintained co-ordinated control, the TV said. That meant they'd shit themselves and done a runner. I thought of how bad things must have been there. What with remission AND parole, cons are not in a hurry to riot. I hoped Jake was enjoying the elation but feared for him come the end of the cons' control of the wing blocks. I waited for the first predictable stories of ringleaders.

By this time me and the Sailor had managed to get on a VTC welding course. That afternoon in the shop I thought of possible solidarity actions, but after talking with a few guys at tea-break it all seemed aggravatingly unrealistic. All I managed was graffitti around the place with a magic marker I'd got my mitts on.

Many weeks later a few Hull cons started to turn up in L-L. Hull was out of action. The screws who'd done a runner when it went off, were cocky and brutal when they'd regained control. One guy who'd been in a wing that hadn't joined the riot told me how they'd ripped up his photos and liquidated his budgie. I was sympathetic but he did go on about that budgie. I wanted to know everything: he just wanted more and more letters written, Parliament, Ombudsman, High Courts, this and that.

"You don't give a monkeys about his budgie," Joe said. "You're like a Trotskyist, you listen to his story but only because you're itching to recruit him."

Joe and I knew each other well by then. He certainly knew how to wind me up. I tried to strangle him and we fell in a heap on the floor of my cell.

"Recruit him to what, you cheeky fucker, " I shouted.

He just laughed like a crazy.

"I am sorry for the geezer and I'm sorry about his budgie, it's just he does go on about it."

"Well you must be a masochist listening. He wasn't even in the riot and he's come out of it all right."

"Easy for you to say, you're not minus a budgie."

We got more substantial news when cons like Attilla the Scouse turned up much later. He'd had three months in a special chokey within the Dartmoor chokey. The Home Office had recreated the conditions of the Special Units which they'd been forced to close down after a lot of protest and the will power of Mickey Williams. This time they'd been crafty; they'd opened no new buildings; given it no name, just imposed a regime of solitary-made-absolute, a planned routine of sensory deprivation.

By this time I'd experienced some minimal sensory deprivation myself and that had been bad enough. The cube-cells of L-L, the non-availabilty of pirated paint to break up the universal white speckle, night after night of it could do funny things to a person. I'd been there about a year when I got this real scare one night. It was in those moments between being awake and being asleep: a blinding rush started from my feet, sped up my body and Boom in the head; a heart attack, cerebral knockout, that was it, curtains. I survived, shaken and next day told Dave what had happened. He'd had the same thing, perversely reassuring. My attack prompted him to investigate and he found it had a name, the K Complex.

"You mean it's known about."

"Yep, enough of an objective fact to satisfy even you. It's the sudden explosion of lots of unused energy, used up in a flash."

He showed me the article and there it was, pinned down by some Austrian doctor years ago. It happened again, still scary enough at the time, just as Larry told me it was always a shock when you stood near an unseen pheasant and it exploded up at you, but not so scary in the minutes after now that it was something known, something that had an explanation. Sure I had lots of unused energy to burn.

As it happened, about the time of Attilla's arrival, the Harrier had decided to while away some more hours on the Open University. He'd gone for a course called the Biological

Basis of Behaviour. It sounded dodgy, Pavlov and manipulation, information only of use to the ruling class.

"Pavlov was just describing the facts," he said. "You can't slag him off just because the facts don't happen to suit you."

"But the facts as you call them came out of a set-up. The dog didn't need the fucking bell to eat his dinner."

"If you want to know how things work you've got to take them apart, experiment, introduce new factors and see what happens when this meets that. Anyway I heard you were at the Rosko Roadshow last night."

It was an outrageous change of tack but it put me on the defensive. It was true, I had gone, it had been the first show in years. Not like the Scrubs where there'd been a few like Kathy Kirby's big night. Rosko, who called himself Emperor Rosko, wasn't a patch on that. He spent a lot of the time handing out stickers like a missionary. I felt defensive because I hadn't even enjoyed it.

"You go on about the liberation of women but there you were, just to see the go-go dancers, how's that for degradation."

I wriggled. I squirmed, but the man was remorseless. In desperation, my motives being so misunderstood, I picked up one of his OU books and opened it at a page headed The Hypothalamus. An amzing part of the brain, very sophisticated. It regulated some basic body processes, the ones we experience as automatic, taking care of themselves. To work it needed stimulus. I wasn't sure what stimulus exactly but got a picture of the ecology of the body, that there was nothing mystical about the effects of sensory deprivation.

So it was that when Attilla, the debonair scouse hard-nut, told me about the regime on the Moor I felt a fresh burst of anger. He told me too that three screws had been well to the fore when it came to handing out stick when they'd regained control of the wing. Batterings; faces slammed down in the porridge, jam and marge; milk pissed in, all while the screws stood round the hotplate thirty-handed with the cons out one at a time. This was before the more leisurely process of smashing, ripping, and killing personal belongings.

I was banged up with my tea after he'd told me all this. The pictures bobbed about in my head and brought back all the frustration I'd felt at the time of the riot itself. I looked at my tea, the bacon that was never quite cooked, the brittle but dense fried bread and the orange-pink stuff called spaghetti which in my preoccupied rage I'd put on my plate. I pictured my face plastered in that, congealed in my hair, stuffed in my earholes. I pictured and remembered the last week's gangster movie we'd seen in the gym.

"How did he make it to be Capo?" the p-and-t man had asked as the Mafia boss got splattered over his pasta in a modest restaurant.

"Just a jumped up torpedo," I said. "The Maf were going through a lean time."

"I didn't know they had lean times."

"Neither did I but it sounded good."

Meanwhile the sharpie who'd pulled off this coup was himself starting to fatten and slacken now that he was off the streets. He wound up copping his chips over a fruit stall, blood and peach juice bursting out over his white suit. Then this staged scene gave way to the immediacy of that Hull hotplate, the shouts and sweat of the screws, the swaying ranks of laughing, growling faces as the lone con went down.

I'd made a resolution not to fall asleep during teatime lock-up on the grounds that I felt so shitty, a dry, dry mouth, giddy and a hovering headache, when I woke up again. Only I did need to lie down. I turned on the radio. A news interviewer was steaming into a shop-steward.

— Don't you realise the effect your action is having on the pound and therefore the cost-of-living for your members?

The steward sounded punch-drunk. The interviewer weighed in again.

— How can you justify this action when your own Union leader, Jack Jones, has described it as irresponsible.

A spark of anger brought the steward back off the ropes.

— Jack Jones should remember that he is paid by us, that he represents us, not the other way round.

Then the News moved seamlessly to the arrival in Plymouth of someone who'd sailed the Atlantic in a craft that was either smaller or more primitive than all the ones that had done it before.

I woke to the click of the lock opening and stayed on the bed, groggy and vulnerable. Ten minutes later I was still there, afraid of the dizziness I might feel if I got up. The spaghetti and fried bread I had not eaten were waving up and down in front of my nose.

"Look at this," I heard and shot up, nauseous. It was Joe.

"What are you doing you fucking madman," I shouted, the voice quavery.

"Look at this man, this is reality. Do you realise that this solid orange chalk which is now stuck to your plate might have been glued in your stomach. And as for this," he said, banging the fried bread on the side of the plate to no effect, "I can only say, you've had a narrow escape."

"What are you trying to do to me?" I asked feebly.

"Me?" Joe said with that dangerously vacant look, "I was merely confirming how wise you were not to put this gluey shit in your stomach. Anyway I've got you woken up and if I was to open this window we might even get rid of this horrible smell."

The window did the trick, I sat up wide awake.

"Good, I've something serious to tell you."

"Who are you, the fucking doctor?"

The thought was unworthy, instead Joe said that some Hull

screws had been posted here and one at least had been an outstanding bastard.

"It's a provocation, one of the Hull boys might blow and they've had enough trouble, weeks, months, years of remission down the drain."

"We'll have to front something up," I said. "There's space to push, I mean there's even a team of cops looking at what the screws done which means it was out of order even by their own standards."

"Mmm. What do you make of this Superintendant Sagar, there's cons wouldn't give a rozzer a dead match talking to him. The Sage, he's thinking about it."

The Sage was another Republican prisoner. He'd been in the riot too and wound up here after a few months touring the chokey facilities of England's local jails. He'd been a PTI in the British army, said employment prospects weren't too hot in Strabane, and had a huge beard in the Karl Marx style. He'd taken up painting and kept at it late in the night. His arrival had doubled the Republican quota on the wing.

"Some of the soundest people we'll ever know are talking to him, there must be something in it. Attilla says the guy is different, really believes in the law, got a down on anyone who breaks it, screws included."

"Hard to believe John."

"A few good apples in the barrel. Anyway it's well out of order sending those screws here, what is this place, a dustbin?"

"So?"

"A sit-down might be possible, nothing too heavy and we might get some support."

"They can take a protest."

"Not here, they don't get many and it might shake up Jack the Governor. Last thing he wants is any bother between him and a smooth climb up the Department ladder."

"OK, worth a go, but this place, it'll be a struggle to pull it off."

"I could do with some adrenalin, half the time I feel I'm coasting through this too easy."

"Is that right. You know who I'd like you to meet?"

"Who, Jill Knight, Melford Stevenson, some hang-em-and-flog-em fanatic?"

"Nope, one of those smug fuckers in remand nicks, the ones write If You Can't Do The Time, Don't Do The Crime on the cell wall."

"Those cunts. All over Brixton that was, easy enough to say on remand, you don't know what The Time is till you've done it."

"You've nearly done yours."

"Nearly is a long time."

By Sunday morning exercise I felt there was a good chance of pulling it off. A few of us had been sounding out a whole range of cons on the Saturday. David had some trouble with a guy going about the fish.

"You remember it, we all agreed we wouldn't take the food, yet some of them took the fish, they ate the fucking fish."

Dave said this had been around seven years before in Strangeways and the guy always brought it up when something was likely to go off. I'd skirted around the subject with a couple of lifers. I had a date, they didn't. At worst I'd lose some remission, for them it might just tip the scales to another x number of years, so I just mentioned what we had in mind, no more. In reality it would depend on how many people took part, if it was over half the nick the chances were there'd be no serious consequences for anyone. It would be down to what happened on the night.

It was going to be after the Sunday evening movie in the gym. Apart from exercise it was the only time the whole jail could be together and there were usually more cons at the film than on exercise. On this Sunday morning the con football team were playing an outside team and there was a good crowd on the touchlines. The Governor was there too with his tweed cap and pipe, like he was a country gent on his estate; Jack's Park, Joe called the exercise field. He was a rugby man but on Sundays he stood there with the Chief like a knowledgeable spectator of football, a man for whom the game belonged to some higher-plane of existence. In some bit of his mind the con became a player for the duration of the match. A couple of weeks before he'd shown his class when a punch-up broke out on the pitch. He'd looked through it as if it weren't really happening, ignoring the disparity between prison rules and the rules of the game. A con had been sent-off, any other situation and it would have been 28 days remission.

This Sunday abuse homed in on the referee after he'd done some finger-waving at Attilla, a rubust centre-forward.

"Rap his knuckles ref."

"Where you from, Wandsworth?"

"UP THE CONVICTS"

"Put him on bread and water you cunt."

Behind the prison team's goal I homed in on an LG I'd known a few years. He was pissed off at being left out of the team. Not a skilful player but he was a fitness fanatic which had to count for something. So I sympathized and put the sit-down idea to him. He was not enthusiastic, it was obvious, just as the visiting team stormed through on goal.

"See no strength in the midfield, no fucking strength."

"Pathetic," I said. "But it's a fucking liberty sending those animals here."

"I agree with you John, don't get me wrong, but there's so many no-good cunts here you'll only get a few backing you."

"Thing is if those screws stay here, it'll go off one day, you know what I mean."

I jumped as the ball flew past my ear from a ferocious off-target shot, but I knew your man was thinking about it.

"Are you going to speak then, you know, tell them what it's all about," he said.

"Yes, I'll do that." We'd struck a deal, his support would mean a good showing from A Wing, from the LGs and a lot more on the strength of that. The visiting team stormed forwards again, only this time the shot was a goal. Your man flung up his hands.

"See what I mean, the geezer fell over, let them in," he said. "Just hasn't got the strength the cunt."

By teatime I felt confident, everyone on our wing knew. A sarcastic conman who claimed to have been a member of the Communist party said, "Going to do a Lenin are you, turn the masses with a speech."

"You won't find me wound up in a mausoleum," I said, feeling good.

The gym was big, not like the packed, smoky Rec of the Scrubs. I sat with David in the second row of chairs. We kept looking round, it looked full enough. Tony Curtis was playing a thirties gangster in a film that had been edited in weird places.

"He's down to B movies now, it'll be TV films next," David said.

I got absorbed in the story in fits and starts. He seemed well too temperamental to be a gang leader. Other faces were less than hearty in their greetings.

Most films were like this but some had touched a nerve. There'd been "State of Siege" which I'd seen legless, through a haze of George's purple beetroot hooch. It was gripping through the haze, I'd sweated with the Tupameros on the bus. Or "The Mean Machine," set in a southern US jail. The cons' Amerian football team overcame death and disfigurement to beat the screws team while Eddie Albert as the Nixon-like psycho football freak went murderously ape-shit. Most of all there was "One Flew Over the Cuckoo's Nest". Me and Jean-Pierre had leaped out of our chairs cheering when the Red Indian finally shows himself and finishes off lobotomized rebel Jack Nicholson. That night only two out of the regular forty went for their evening tot of tranquilizer, that's what I was told.

This film tonight though was staple diet. Things were looking worse for Tony Curtis. He was looking isolated and was living on a misplaced lazy confidence, too much wishful thinking. What's more the poor sod was in love. Personally I think being in love is pretty fucking amazing but when you're in his kind of business, bit of a luxury. Meanwhile the cops were closing the net.

It started to get to me, worried about our own show. It wasn't about remission or anything, but that it might be a shambles: that I might stumble over my words; that at the decisive moment it just wouldn't happen, that there'd be just a few of us left with the choice of creeping sheepishly out, or getting well fucked over. Back on the screen your man was captured in a deserted fairground, still in love.

It's an electric chair job and the Director loves it. The sequence goes on and on, chaplains, governors, legalities, while your man is absolutely on his own on his own in this dark, private and ordered thing. It's obviously end of the film, why don't they just finish it so we can get started. But no, this fucking director lingers over the chair itself. Close-ups of the straps as your man is strapped in, the crinkle and crackle of the leather loud from the screen. ZAP goes the voltage. No one in the whole gym can be feeling good. Tony Curtis looks as white as a sheet ready for the laundry, his body flung about in the confines of the chair.

The lights went up. We looked around. A few cons at the back got up and left, not so many. The LG footballer said from behind, "This is fucked John, no good."

But there were half the cons of the jail still sat there, it was OK. It would not have been OK if there'd been a long wait. We were lucky the screws had an AG on the scene in quick time.

"Go on then John," I heard from behind.

As per usual there was plenty of unnecessary, unwanted adrenalin pumping around to go with the dry mouth. I said something to the effect that there were some Hull screws here who were liable to face charges and that they were a provocation. I did not sound eloquent. Worse, I repeated myself, could hear myself doing it. Still when I sat down there were cries of, That's right Governor. Then an ex-Hull con took up the point, we wanted them out at least until whatever Hull screws were going on trial went on trial. The AG came right out and said that he couldn't get rid of screws on our say-so, who did we think we were, but that on the other hand he would pass on our complaints.

"We've made our point," I heard from behind. That was it, a shuffling of chairs and feet. It was over and felt like a ludicrous anti-climax. It was level-headed Dave who said it was fine, what had I expected, mass fucking insurrection?

He was right. It had been just solid enough, two days later the screws we'd named were gone.

Leisure Hours, Hard Hours

I WAS TALKING to Kenny in the kitchen. He was a guy you couldn't miss. He didn't wear the nick-issue, blue-and-white striped shirt with PT shorts, socks and boots as a one-off, as a grab for status as a character. He didn't need it, was a 45 year old Scotsman, a veteran of security jails. No, he wore them all the time, on the wing, at work, when it was hot and when it was cold. The only time I saw him wearing trousers it turned out he was ill.

It was about half seven in the evening, a quiet time down

there. The kitchen was only the width of a four-ring cooker, about seven foot long, with a narrow slatted shelf running along it at sitting height. I was sat there with a jug of tea in my hand while Kenny told me about his first parole review, the one with the Local Review Committee. I'd never applied for parole, for me it was a pointless wind-up but I knew how the routine worked. This committee was made up of concerned local worthies.

"They boggled at the shorts," I said.

Kenny looked at me like I was really dumb. "It wasn't the shorts man, you've got to have the whole picture. I went in after this div has been pounding the guy's ears for an hour. The complete life-story."

"So you were the light relief, a bold tactic."

"Why don't you stop interrupting. I just went in with the Mao book under my arm and said, Hi I'm Hans Coco-Pops, how you doing and that."

I laughed till I could feel warm tears dribbling from my eyes. Then I heard myself, the laughter sounded dangerously crazy. I had to put the tea down. A screw idling at the other end of the hot-plate glared at me. Kenny glared too, he wasn't finished. "I could see it in his face," he said, "How's this headbanger slipped through the filter, like I'd gatecrashed a Cabinet meeting."

The bastard had set me off again. Another screw came out the office to give me a glare and my stomach was in bits.

"But I'll give him his due," Kenny said, "he flicked through my file and asked the usual questions just like an old trouper."

"The show must go on," I said.

"The show does go on," he said, grabbing my jug of tea and taking a swig. "I was on this wing once, the island it was, and there was this AG, he was never off it. Never had a home to go to, he was creeping about all hours."

"How's about you give me my tea back."

"How's about you leave me alone, I'm trying to tell you about this AG. I was on the book and you'll know how it is in some of them, they have an AG with them for one of the hourly spy-hole checks."

"Sure I remember, it was the one with all the whispering."

"So if it's normal, one AG will do it once every five days. Not this bastard, he was in every night."

As he spoke I looked out the window towards the extra bit of fencing that protected the gatehouse. In the floodlights it looked like a Prisoner of War movie.

"I've often wondered what those Home Office cretins put in his report."

"Whose?"

"Fucks sake, are you deaf? I'm talking about this AG. Now did his report say he showed a real devotion to his work. Or did it say, This guy is a perverted creep who should not advance beyond his present grade."

"An interesting question," I said and tried to focus on it.

All that was held up by the arrival of the Wee Man from the Falls Road, one more Republican on the wing. The whole kitchen started to rattle. I tried to cling on to my thoughts about this AG and lost them as the Wee Man started to talk in his normal voice. The ladle and slice danced on their hooks.

"Have you got a few wee eggs old buddy," he began, looking me straight in the eyes with a big grin on his chops.

"I have got eggs yes," I said cautiously.

"How's about I cook an omelet my mate," he said giving me a huge wink, not just the eye but his whole fucking head.

"Sure, there's some in my cell, take what you want. You've got cheese to go with it," I said.

"I can always get some," he said. He turned to Kenny. "Can you give us a wee bit of marge?"

"You're some fucking hustler," I said shaking my head in admiration though I'm not sure that's what I felt. "I mean you come down here with sweet fuck-all and before we know where we are you're coming out with giant omelets, giant omelets from wee eggs."

The wee man's grin never faltered. If anything it grew broader.

"Aye, you can have a bit of marge," Kenny said.

"My advice is to get some cheese then we're in business," I said. "And how could you fail with your charm."

"Charm," Kenny said, his incredulity cartooned. "It's more like a pick-axe handle through the glass. No, I know who you are, you're the one at the shotgun wedding with the shotgun, telling the groom it's all for his own good."

"Aye I'm some pup," the Wee Man said, he was delighted.

He left, leaving the ladle and slice to bounce to a stop. I looked out through the wire-glass of the kitchen on to the wing. A screw had just arrived through the wing with a con pushing a trolley with an urn of official tea and what were called jam scones. The con was a rare nonce, Straffen, one with status, he'd done decades of bird, done super-security wings and had a child-like face under a tall bald head, a dead ringer for the ancient retainer. Kenny and I were still shell-shocked from the Wee Man's visit but were struggling doggedly back to where we'd been. I'd just got there when the tannoy started up.

DOWNSTAIRS FOR SUPPER
SUPPER IS ON THE WING

Dogged nothing, this was swimming the channel with the sea turned to tapioca.

"What you were saying about the AG and reports on him," I began slowly. "In the first place it assumes the Home Office have spies, that they keep tabs on their own, but it's more than that, I can't see them being able to write down that he was a pervert. It would undermine their whole position to even think in those terms. They need to believe in their own righteousness however diabolical it is, know what I mean. It's how the British Empire worked."

Two cons came into the kitchen to make their own tea with real tea leaves. I got off the bench, wary of a dose of boiling water on the knees. Outside a few cons came down for supper. Some took nick-tea, others looked at the scone, trying to hold off what they already knew, that it was the same old soggy shit that tasted bicarbonate.

"It's like this," Kenny said, bringing me back again, "there's a difference between what they say in public and what they say behind locked doors. Like the report on Hull riot."

"Yes. So?"

More cons came in to use the boiler. Next to it was written A HULL SCREW WITHOUT HIS RIOT STICK IS A WANKER, a legacy of my magic-marker. It had faded in the steam. The throng of cons squeezed us up against the furthest wall. We adjourned to the hotplate.

"In the report," Kenny said, intent, "they put the whole thing down to two prime-movers, right? Can you seriously see two guys setting off a riot in any jail these days. Nobody's going to riot unless things are really desperate."

"Yes. And?"

"They're saying that in public but even those Home Office zombies must want to know the real score."

Larry, the p-and-t man, came hurrying past for a jug of nick-tea from the urn.

"Joined the hotplate hangers-on," he said. "Another couple of ghosts, I never thought I'd see the day. Here, you're not in for noncing are you?"

He was so far into this line of abuse that he did not notice the jug was full.

"Shit, there's tea all over my foot," he shouted.

"Turn the fucking thing off you cretin," Kenny shouted back as the puddle of tea moved swiftly towards his feet.

"Stay cool man, this floor could do with a good clean, this tea's the very stuff for the job."

"Lets try again," I said as Larry hurried off, well pleased with himself. "Perseverance will be rewarded."

"That's what I tell myself every night."

"In one way you're right," I said confidently. "They must have been told that the very niggling and screw-down they'd given the green light to, that it was building up the aggravation. But from their point of view it would all be justified as Good Order or Security, you see what I mean."

"As a matter of fact no, I don't."

"Those notions justify everything to them, and at certain points it outweighs them wanting to know, or being capable of knowing what really happened. They have to see everything as a conspiracy."

"Why?"

The screw who'd given me the glare had got bored and started to talk to his pal in the Control Centre through the speaker on the far wall which was normally used to open gates. I did not like this screw. We'd been stuck between two gates once and I could see the bastard start to sweat, a claustrophobic screw.

"Well, in Ireland they couldn't admit that all the people of Anderstown say, hated their guts, so they put it down to a few psychopaths and introduced internment, thinking there'd be no comebacks."

"No, these bastards know what they're doing, they've been at it for centuries. Stamp down hard, that's how the British Empire worked."

"Sure, but they make mistakes. They'd like us to believe they're infallible but they make mistakes and half the time it's because they can't believe there's masses of people against them."

"No, they don't teach that at Eton. They know most people

are against them, they learn to hang on to what they've got, they've money tied up in it."

"OK, but what I'm saying is they like to get their rents nice and regular AND feel righteous about it, bequeathing democratic constitutions to the natives and all that shit."

The duty SO had got bored, come out of his office and stood at the end of the hotplate. We went quiet and the screw promptly stopped rabbitting into the box. A con looked out of the kitchen, he said there was only one ring working on the cooker. The SO was in his element, he had a problem to deal with. He knew how bad it was, he said, had done his best. He would have the electrician over tomorrow. Maybe tonight even.

They're just bigger crooks than us," Kenny said. "They've got more dough tied up in it and more front."

"You're right about the front. Like that Labour bastard going on about tightening your belt, pulling up your trousers, before rushing off to his two hundred grand farm. Sure there's all that but they like to feel good about it, they like to feel it's their right, the power and the means of production."

I felt a sudden draft in the air. The Wee Man was back with the means of production for an omelet.

"Don't crowd me," he said, giving big licks to the actual production, dropping the beaten eggs into the frying pan with a flourish. The geezer who'd been cooking on the only working ring but had been sucked into conversation with the SO, couldn't believe what he was seeing. Now there was no free ring at all, let alone four. The Wee Man deftly transferred the pan to the grill. It was not strictly an omelet, the cheese on top fluffed up under the grille.

"That's some omelet," the Wee Man said like we all needed ear-trumpets.

"Lets go down to my cell with it," Kenny said. "What's the time anyway?"

"Plenty of time, it's only half eight."

The SO must have heard me, he was cued back to his office for another go on the tannoy.

DOWNSTAIRS FOR TREATMENTS
DOWNSTAIRS FOR TREATMENTS

Kenny's cell was neat and austere. We ate the omelet quickly. "So there you've got it," he said. "Money and power in a situation where power is money."

"But they still make out they're doing us a favour by owning all those productive forces and investing now and then. They invest to make money, but they make out it's just to make jobs for people who otherwise wouldn't have them. Not that they go on about the virtues of capitalism so much these days."

I stopped a moment, all sorts of things I'd been thinking for weeks were coming out.

"They've had to change the tune a bit. Now it's more like how all that economic growth was temporary, can't take it for granted. So they just go on about the mechanics of everything and you're supposed to feel good just because you know which particular stroke they've pulled. Just the mechanics, not what it's for. The means justify the means. It's like security: security for who, for what, they don't ask that."

"Aye, security's their answer for everything," the wee man bellowed. "I can't have a photo taken to send to my girl because it's against security."

"An alibi for every occasion," Kenny said. "You see how much money they've invested in security here. What was that rat's name?"

"Which particular rat did you have in mind?"

"The one with the two hundred grand farm."

"Dennis Healey."

"Aye, Healey with his spending cuts. You can see them here, little by little, less classes, the food a bit worse, but they've still the money for security, yon cameras by the crateful."

"The laugh is, the more security toys they've got, the more scared they are of the place going up and all that stuff getting mangled."

Kenny laughed. "But in the cuts they did increase spending in a couple of areas one of which happened to be money for screws' overtime. And how was it packaged, Necessary For Security."

The wee man, in an unusually normal voice, said they'd manufactured security problems to get it. "It was headlines in 'The Sun', they needed it to protect us Republicans from other prisoners."

"Jesus Christ," Kenny said. He was outraged.

"I don't need any protection and I don't need theirs. They're the ones doing the stirring, they're the ones giving the beatings."

The tannoy crackled into life.

END OF ASSOCIATION

END OF ASSOCIATION

I went upstairs to my own cell and then to a recess with a jug for water. There was a big fight on the radio that night. Mr Big, a new LG on the spur, he was saying, "You know how it'll go, the Yank will be cagey for a few rounds then he'll fold, that's what he's there for."

"No way," the Sailor said.

It was still going strong on the spur. "I tell you what, I'll give you Three to One if you take the Yank, you can't get fairer than that."

I was tidying my cell when the wee man burst in. "You got any sugar old buddy?"

My reply wasn't fast enough, he was into his stride.

"We're all good socialists together, my mate."

I laughed. I liked it. "Far be it from me to say we're not all socialists together, we do our best. Thing is, the only time you mention it's when you want something off me."

"That's terrible cynical old buddy. You know me, I'm not like that," he said with a grin and wink that nearly took his head off.

"All I'm saying is that it's a pleasure, a real pleasure to give you sugar, it's just I could do without the spiel."

"That's true socialism."

"Something like that," I said, my usual pedantry holding me back from any generalisations on the strength of a bit of sugar ration.

After he'd gone I closed my door. I hadn't used to do it, too much like being my own jailer; lately it felt better that way, keeping the bastards out of my life that bit more.

I lay on the bed and heard the electronic lock clicking on each door in sequence. One, two three, then mine, and on down the spur. My decompression chamber, letting all the bits and pieces of the day drain out, a transition period between the buzz of the wing and this solitude. Most times I enjoyed solitude, a creative time for thinking things right through. This time my head threw up pictures of my first days inside, in Brixton. They seemed a long way off but closer than some more recent times. I remembered an old boy telling me some of the basics. Do one day at a time, he'd said. In a way he was right: please deliver me from all those equations and calculations; like three-quarters of the sentence done and it will be four fifths soon and then I'll only have to do a quarter of what I've already done. Please deliver me from those and a quarter of what I've done already, that's anyway a long fucking time. But living one day at a time, that's hard too, every day a new improvisation.

I looked out of the window, it's size and height the only decent thing about the cell. The sun was to the left of the sky I could see, it was big and red. I switched off the cell light. A cone-shaped mass of cloud opening upwards and towards me, moved slowly leftwards. The setting sun made the clouds into embers, one side pinky-red, the other greying up. On the pink side of the cone there was some clear sky with one or two sharply defined, delicate smaller clouds. Slowly, slowly the grey took over the pink space, and the heart of the cone blackened. There were bars between me and the window but I could open the window, tilting it out to nearly 45 degrees. I balanced my chin on the middle bar and pushed my nose out under the top one. I breathed in deeply that summer-night air which is so good, so unmistakable; the air of nights when you can walk the streets with no particular place to go

A familiar worm slides into my head: I'm so conscious of how good it is, too conscious. It's spoiling it isn't it, a voice says. It's putting another set of bars, another pane of glass between you and the here and now. In response I swivelled my chin again. The light was still so clear out left, the upper halves of three conifer trees and a water tower were in perfect focus above the perimeter wall. All so familiar. As is the constant jet of steam coming out of a pipe on top of the Laundry building which is dead centre in my fixed range of vision. It's always coming out as a jet and dispersing further out into the sky, the jet still coming. I turned my head rightwards again, the grey had eaten most of the pink and was being eaten in turn by the following blackness. I turned again, the conifers were blurring, only the steam-jet was constant.

With the darkness comes back today and tomorrow and a familiar depression. Every question that should be political becomes one of self, of whether or not I lived up to my standards, to the way I see myself. In Long Lartin the screws are really into using christian names, John this and John that. It makes me tense up. They're so fucking persistent with it but I should have snarled at that bastard today. I should have done. Everytime they use my christian name and get away with it, I'm compromised.

— It's hard to snarl all the time.

— You don't believe that, it's just an excuse. You should slag them off so decisively that it'll never happen again.

— But I can't live off bitterness and rage, it's too damaging.

— You slippery bastard, more excuses and they're what really damage you.

I needed a break from this never-ending dialogue. I'd been hearing the roars and shouts from dozens of radios and switched mine on. The Brit was getting hammered by combination punches from the Yank. The commentator was surprised, the Brit had been so much on top. I turned the radio off again. I wanted to write a letter, just get into it, something which the voice of pure-motives-and-misery couldn't put down though it did try.

— It'll just be a load of bollox, you'll give the impression of being on top of things but you're not really. It'll just be a load of abstract analysis. Big deal.

I sighed so loud I could hear it. It's true that if I was feeling low I wouldn't write about it, not with the censors reading it. You have to make a decison early on about your letter-writing, either you write more or less what you want or not at all. My mate Phil, bookie and wall-artist won't write at all but I see that as a defeat, amplifying the isolation. Anyway for now mine are full of Marxist analysis. No apologies for that, it's good stuff, just the writing is getting smaller and smaller. I figure either the screw-censor has given up reading them or will burst in my cell one day shouting, You're confusing Rate of Surplus Value with Rate of Profit you fool. No, that's not true, I don't believe it at all, he's just given up.

I picked up my biro and the voice made one last effort.

So you've analyzed it all but it's still going to be a lie, hiding your misery.

— Fuck you voice of self-hatred. What do you think I am,

superman.

This anger helped me back to the six-by-four inch, lined paper. I clawed my way to think creatively, exhilarated by the effort to describe exactly what I felt about a piece I'd heard on the radio called 'Judgement'. It was two hour monologue and I'd been gripped right through. The speaker was a Red Army Officer on trial. He'd been one of seven captured by the Germans in Poland and then left naked in a cellar with no food or water, and no possible exit, when the

German army had to beat a sudden retreat.

When the advancing Russian army discovered the cellar they found two survivors and a lot of bones. One survivor is mad, the other, the speaker, gives an account of what happened. In the cellar he had never thought of having to justify himself, but at the moment he sees the cellar with the eyes of the liberators he knows he will have to do this. It was precisely his sanity, the coherence of his explanation which so appalled those sitting in judgement. He describes the dignity of the collective decision for cannibalism and the courage of one Rubin to be the one who smothers and cuts up the body of the first volunteer. But it has cost him. Rubin is the mad survivor. The speaker who has initiated nothing is the strong one at the end, full of admiration for Rubin, caring for him. Slowly it becomes clear that the judges are understanding, absolving, sympathizing with the speaker. At the same time they are utterly repulsed.

When I'd finished describing the story I suddenly felt how chill the air had become and heard the wind. The scene through the window had changed, the clouds black and serious. Delicate slivers of rain hit the window till it all let go in a proper rainstorm. I stood up and stretched across the table to put my face to the bars and waited ten, twenty seconds till the rain released the rich heavy smell of earth from the hard summer ground and reached my nose. I breathed deep till it hit my diaphragm like the first roll-up after a tobacco drought. The tiredness of my eyes, crusted and heavy, dissolved. I concentrated on the sounds, each individually audible at the window: the spongy, hissing rhythm of rain on grass; water running out of the gutter and down the drainpipe; the random sucks and whooshes of the wind.

Let it happen. Let it happen.

The letter took off again, a continual nervous excitement. The radio drama had struck many chords. The notion that who we really are being revealed in extreme, desperate situations seemed all too pat for those who'd never been in such situations. Such experiences would very likely exhaust our psychic stamina and would leave the survivors separated, cut off from other people. I thought of my dad. He'd been sixteen or seventeen in the trenches of the First World War, the experience took something away from him, cut him off.

At the end I felt a deep but momentary satisfaction from having thought something through, right through to what I thought of hunger strikes. But there was also the adrenalin that went with it. So much of it sloshing around in my head, its bitter residue biting my stomach. A fixed chemical battle between it and my sense of satisfaction as so many times before.

Feeling comfortable in bed was an ally to the sense of satisfaction, but this time the sheets were at the end of their seven day span. I could feel the crumbs embedded in them. I leaped out of bed in irritation, stretched the bottom sheet and swept it with the back of my other hand. As I got back into bed I wiped the soles of my feet on top of the single blanket. Shit, the sheets weren't even cool. I pictured a woman friend, tried to feel her reality, he face mobile as it is, tried to imagine her not in my imagination, to feel her warmth. I concentrated on the picture, stroking my cock. But it broke up and became a cartoon woman, huge and pink.

— Jesus Christ, will it never end?

— It' will, under 2 years if nothing drastic happens.

— Two years, how can you talk so lightly of 2 years. God it's hot again. It wasn't the right sort of rain. I've mistimed going to sleep.

The right time for going to sleep had got to be such a delicate business. If I tried too early I'd get restless, too late like now, and I'd be overtired.

— You've got to let yourself go, you're trying to grab at sleep, it doesn't work.

— That doesn't help.

— You should have stuck with the Yoga. That's your problem, no discipline. The only way now is to let go.

— That's like telling someone on high scaffolding who's afraid of heights and has frozen, that they've got to relax. A lot of fucking help that is.

— Rationalise, rationalise, it's the only thing you're any good at.

The spyhole cover rose and fell, the first time I'd noticed the screw on his hourly round this night. I tried a childhood trick and turned over the pillow. The other side was cool. Then it wasn't cool. I focussed on the park of my childhood, one I hadn't seen in years, made myself a map and walked it out. Across the iron bridge over the railway sidings, on past the ash tree, along the upward curve to the playground. Left or right? I chose the left path up past the park-keepers' hut.

GzzzzzzGzzzzz, some distant insane buzzing, a radio in some far-off cell, maybe thirty yards away. I turned on mine. Shit, after midnight, I'd missed John Peel and now it was some creep on Radio Two. I switched it off. The delinquent radio had got worse, a DJ talking in words I couldn't hear.

— So what happened to the park then?

— It was that poxy radio.

— Bollox, I bet no one else can even hear it. It's just an

excuse, you weren't really picturing that park, you just can't concentrate.

— Thanks pal. It's sexual repression, enforced abstinence, it makes concentration impossible, Reich said so.

— Oh that's all right then is it. As long as it's not your fault it doesn't matter that you can't concentrate.

— It's not a matter of fault, it's not being able to do what I want to do. I'm not in charge of myself.

The DJ was back through a scrambler. This was torture. Up and down waves of non-words. Torture, on a par with the clicking pipes of Brixton. On a par with a fucking screech-owl that had been hanging around a month back. Couldn't find a mate obviously, just screeched for hours on end. I ended up waiting for its next screech like I'd waited for the pipes to click.

— Look pal the Home Office didn't put that owl there with the express purpose of driving round the twist. You're so egocentric you paranoiacs.

— I know it wasn't put there Slippery, it screeched because that's the way those fucking owls are. And I'm not paranoid. Mind you with those Brixton pipes I had my suspicions.

— There you are, you've admitted it, you are paranoid.

— I'm not saying they rigged it up but once they knew about it, and there were enough complaints, they weren't in a hurry to do anything, they didn't do anything. Like the oil companies and the OPEC price rise.

— There you go again, if it moves, analyze it.

I turned over on to my back.

— You know you can't sleep on your back, you're just delaying it.

— But things can change, I can change my life, I can, I'll learn to sleep on my back. Anyway it feels more peaceful.

It did too. I rubbed my hand up and down the cool, roughish brick wall. The only wall in the cell that isn't bland.

My hand felt the contours and its own smoothness. It felt like a brush.

— See, I've made no effort to put the light on again. I'm trying to sleep. I am trying.

Even the fucking wall set me off again. How depressed I'd been when I arrived at L-L, the smallness, the blandness of the cell. Even the wall panel had caused aggravation. There were times when the computer fucked up without warning. There I'd be, thirsty, reaching for my jug, empty.

No problem I'd press the button and get some from the recess. Nothing happened. Misplaced trust in the computer.

This train of thought made me think it might be worth going out now. It was well after the rush hour between ten and eleven when the light in the box would stay Amber for ages. It would be easy now. I could wash my face in cold water. Out of nowhere came a positive thought. I made a resolution, when I was free I would never stay somewhere I didn't want to be, would never stay somewhere out of inertia or not knowing how to make an exit.

— Yes that's good, that's positive, but then prison must teach you something.

I flung off the sheet and leaped off the bed, pressed the button and the light came on Green immediately. The door clicked open. I walked down the empty, silent spur with a towel. They had a screw stationed on each landing every night. There he was on the other side of the meshed glass just before the recess. His table was covered with shiny porn magazines. I looked again. Fucks sake, the bugger was asleep. The cheek of it, he was doing a job, getting a salary and there he was, spark out.

In the recess I filled a basin with cold water and stuck my head in. Cool. Cool. I rubbed down slowly with the towel. Back in the cell I lay on top of the bed.

— You won't sleep like that, you'll have to get under that

sheet sometime.

— But it feels good.

— Feels good? You might as well get under that sheet now.

BARKER, ARE YOU BACK IN YOUR CELL

My heart bounced as the metallic words boomed round the tight confines of the cell. It was like those bloody pheasants again, I knew what it was but still my heart bounced. I hadn't gone through the motions of locking myself back in again which involved pushing another button in the box and twisting it.

OK I surrender, I shouted back into the box and made the appropriate moves. A white light came on, recognition that I'd made the right moves and was safely banged-up. I lay back on the bed, I was serious, I got under the sheet, remembering to wipe the soles of my feet on top of it. I hated myself for being so feeble. Such a drama out of nothing. I wasn't in the trenches, I didn't face cannibalism or death. Fucks sake, I never used to be like this. In Brixton the cell had often been plunged into darkness at ten but I'd fallen to sleep easily enough. Even when the jury'd been out deciding my future three nights running I'd been asleep in minutes.

OK, I had to stay calm. Try a book. I picked up a Dashiell Hammett off the floor. It was all fucking words. I tried to get involved. One man was trying to clean up a corrupt city. Bollox. One man? Who was he kidding.

I stretched up and switched off the light. I tried another technique and pictured an apple. I concentrated on that apple. A deep, shiny green, the bendy stalk on top so different to the round hardness like an afterthought.

— There you go again, analyzing.

I swiped the voice away and got back to the apple, the green, the deep green, the roundness, the fresh crunch of teeth in the green...

I WOKE UP with the morning click of the lock feeling wide awake and tired. Downstairs at the hotplate it was baked beans. I'd pick some up for the Sage. Kenny was at the head of the queue. I heard him say, "Give me the stoat's beans."

Who was the stoat?

"Who's the stoat?" the hotplate screw asked.

"How the fuck do I know who the stoat is," Kenny said.

I laughed and laughed and felt ten times better.

I saw him again for a talk on Saturday afternoon exercise. It might be summer but the field was close to empty, as many screws as cons. A couple of groups walked laps, three guys played football by some goalposts and Irish Dave was at the wall of the wing nearest the field entrance. The Irish guys had made it a handball wall. There were no regular players out but Dave had found someone to teach. A smashing guy, he could generate excitement into any handball game.

I felt good, Saturday mornings could be a luxury just as they'd been on the out. The Sage had brought me weekend cornflakes in bed. I'd read a bit, dozed, then Jean-Pierre had come by with a luxurious cup of heavy instant coffee before we ambled down to the prison library.

Out on exercise I asked Kenny if he fancied walking a few laps, how I'd been thinking over our talk the other evening.

"What was that now?"

"You know whether the Home Office, the ruling class in general, whether they can really know the truth, whatever they say in public."

"Aye, I remember and him with his fucking omelet, the Wee Man. Well it's fucking obvious, they want to know what is happening and con the public at the same time."

The screw at the corner of the field looked bored to death. In his dark uniform and military-style cap he resembled an insect in the sun. Maybe the Home Office had noticed, they were introducing a new light-blue uniform that made them look like uptight airplane stewards.

"How could they con the public with a zombie like that," Kenny said, eyes on the same screw.

"They do try. Haven't you seen those adverts in the papers, an interesting, challenging job."

The next screw along the perimeter fence had the PO for company. The PO had a walkie-talkie strapped to his chest like it was a medal.

"Why bother," Kenny said. "Why not just say it's a doddle with total job security and unlimited overtime. They'd get all the screws they want with that."

"So you're backing what I'm saying. The fact that they don't put it that way means they can't admit or can't even see what a scabby job it is."

They can see all right, they despise the average screw, just look at this Governor."

"Lord of the Manor."

"Spends more time on a parole punter than them, the screws don't like him. The problem for the working class," he said suddenly, "is that they're always underestimating the viciousness of the ruling class, you saw that programme about Attica."

I had seen it. Horrifying. In my own personal catalogue of horror on a par with the Irish Free State bumping off Republican prisoners not because of what they'd done, but as reprisals.

"And it happens because the working class haven't experienced such viciousness in themselves."

Who would want to.

"I mean I know plenty of nasty guys," he said, "a few drinks inside them and they're bastards but it's always spur of the moment, they don't plan it all out."

A memory of something I'd read recently swam up to the surface.

"You remember Goddard, the judge who had people topped left, right and centre in the fifties?"

"What do you think, you bum. I was in the prime of my youth, you'd have been only in short caiks. Course I remember the old bastard."

"I read this review of a book about him, written long after he was dead of course, when it was years too late to make any difference, and you know what it said?"

"No," Kenny said. His voice was weary.

"When he was about seven or eight years old and it was him was in short trousers, he used to do a little party piece. He put a little piece of black cloth on his head and recited the death sentence."

Kenny stopped. He was horrified, I could see it on his face. My horror too, it grabbed me after I'd spoken the words.

"And the pervert turned his fantasy into reality, Jesus Christ. Having guys killed, quivering in their cells. And the fifties, not so long ago from where I am."

We walked on quietly, it was like I hadn't really understood it, that this was as sick as you could get, till I'd said it.

"I'll tell you a more recent one," Kenny said after a while. "There's a guy due for a five stretch. In the mitigation his brief tells the judge that his client's got cancer and is only expected to last a year or so. You know what the judge says."

"It's got to be Melford Stevenson and I'm not sure I want to know."

"Not bad," Kenny said. "Jackpot. Melford gave him the five stretch and says, Do as much as you can. Now that's how the British Empire was built."

"Yes and what I'm saying is, and it's even worse, I'm saying that they're self-righteous with it."

We were back at the handball wall. From a window the voice of a TV tennis commentator blasted out. He was going spare. WHAT A RALLY. Twice, three times he said it like he was convincing himself.

"So it's me who was right," Kenny said. "In public they say what a great and thankless task the screw is doing while in private they think he's a fucking cretin."

"Yes, I suppose so. I guess even in Ireland they had to change pretty fast. I mean they must have learned from Vietnam that bullshitting yourself doesn't work. Mind you their Intelligence guys had good reason to give them only what they wanted to hear."

"Why's that?"

"All the CIA guys who were telling them Mao was sure to win in China from 1946 onwards, they all got the sack for being right."

"Shooting the messenger, bad policy," Kenny said.

"Anyway what happened to that pervert of an AG you were talking about?"

"The cunt got promoted."

We stopped at the khasi to roll up cigarettes. As we finished I noticed the camera on a nearby column swivel round and point straight at us. I pointed it out.

"Well there's my parole up the spout, you're a liability," Kenny said laughing.

"Says a lot for my conversation then."

The camera began to swivel up and down on its other axis. It was going crazy, up and down, up and down. I looked at my pumps. Nothing out of the ordinary.

"The screw in the Control Room, he's bored," Kenny said.

"No it's your knees," I said, desperate to get away from the horror of judges.

After another lap Kenny said that in spite of my interesting conversation he felt able to drag himself away to catch the end of the tennis. Dave's handball pupil had gone in as well so I asked for a game. There was a chalk line running along the brick wall about two feet off the ground.

You had to hit the ball with an open hand either on the volley or after one bounce and it had to hit the wall above the line. When playing singles practical etiquette demanded aiming for the middle of the wall otherwise there'd be few rallies.

I threw the ball in for Dave to serve. If the server didn't like the bounce of the thrown ball he could reject it. Dave hit my first throw in straight and hard. I hit one straight back dipping just over the line. Dave came in and played one short. I rushed in and got the ball up but he was waiting, his return looped over my head. I chased back and got a touch but no more than that. By the end of the first session of his five serves Dave was Four-One up.

"Negligible," he said. "I can just see you going Six-Four up on your service.

A SUPERB PASSING SHOT, WHAT DELICACY OF TOUCH, the commentator said.

At Five-Three to Dave, my third serve was just below the line. I knew it and he knew it.

"An ace," I cried, "look, it's knocked up chalk."

"It was three bricks under, look at the angle."

"It's the penalty we pay, us players who go for winners."

BORG HAS THREE SET POINTS

"I'll tell you what, I'll give you the point.," I said.

"No, we'll replay it."

"It's yours, I insist."

We grinned at each other and the commentator said how dignified Nastase was in losing the set.

This where you pull back," Dave said. "Two points, a mere trifle, means nothing at this stage of the game."

The game went to eleven points with a clear two point lead needed to win. I blew it when I put a ball up on the roof. It involved a two point loss, practical etiquette, it was aggravation enough to get the PTI screw to get the balls down for this unofficial game. We had just the one ball left, the pupil having put the rest of them up there. So we played Dave's match point with this last ball as the screws started moving in. We dragged it out, hitting straight at a good height.

"The tension is unbearable," I shouted with my tenth shot.

The screws were hovering with intent. The rhythm got faster. I played my last two shots lying on the deck near the wall. The third one I dived for and missed completely.

"A pity the crowd was so small for such a cliffhanger," I said.

"They'll be back for more."

The commentator said it was becoming a formality for Borg. On the way back through the corridors I thought what a great play-leader Dave would be. I didn't normally think like this, didn't think about whether me or any other con should be in or out, unless it was Dick McKilkenny, crudely fitted up for the Birmingham pub bomb, because it seemed futile.

I slept well that night after a sweaty dance in the cell to the music of the Feelgoods and Toots and the Maytals. I didn't notice any of the screw's spyflap checks. If he was going to put on my record that I was a nutter, I didn't give a fuck.

AGGRAVATION

B Y EARLY 1977 I'd got a five stretch under the belt, and some. The days went quickly, the weeks did not. Weird, like there were twenty per week. There was a chance Hilary might get some parole. I lived out that excitement by proxy; felt it too when I was taken to Holloway for an inter-prison visit. After an initial battle to have one at all, we'd had them all too irregularly over the years, always her coming to see me as I was on the A book.

I'd never bothered much with formal attempts to better my situation but one time, bored and fed up, I'd got worked up about Category A and wrote to the European Court of Human Rights. In reality it was an additional punishment I said, a punishment which had not been imposed by the courts. A clown called McNulty wrote back after a few months and said it was none of their business. That wound me up enough for a go at the British courts. A sympathetic lawyer tightened up my argument and cited cases where other instances of administrative punishment had been spotlighted. It looked good, only the Law Society didn't fancy financing the case out of legal aid. Bunch of pricks, end of story, that's how it looked. A couple of weeks later I was called down to the office. The bright SO, the problem-solver, told me I was off the book at last, an administrative decision. My take was cynical, the way the courts were dishing out bird at the time, there was going to be a run on Cat A cells.

It got me my first trip outside since the day I'd come here, a trip to Holloway. In a van, three screws, me cuffed up to the one of them. A light mist lay on the fields. Over half of an hour it gave way to a bright, clear light. There were trees everywhere, fat ones, thin ones, tall and short, all reassuring with their grounded stillness. Nearly naked too, just starting to bud, the intricacy of their branches and twigs sharply focussed. My sense of wealth and wonder cut out the chatter of the screws until we hit London, the London that stretches along the A40, small factories, art deco company HQs and diesel-smoked semis. When we finally got choked up at Hangar Lane exhaust fumes seeped into the van and my bladder began to nag. By the time we got to the Marylebone Road it was torture, bursting for a piss in a gas chamber. I hankered for a siren-wailing police car that would slice us through the mass of metal cars between me and Holloway and squeezed my thighs tight, tried to concentrate on familiar sights and the pavement bustle. By Regents Park knots of tall Arabs in beautiful white robes battled against the wind, the laundry bills had to be ferocious. A steady pain opened up in my kidneys. I couldn't hold out, it wasn't possible. My take on what I saw got more sour by the moment, it was nothing but an obstacle between me and a piss. There was something about the traffic jams of the Euston Road; where nothing moves when the lights are green, that mocked the very notion of revolutionary change. A fact of life; so it was in 1971, so it was in 1977 and so it will be. The Cally Road was an endless stretch of drab and kidney damage was on the cards. Then I noticed the screw I was cuffed up, that he was agitated. The symptoms were clear, two of us wriggling and hunched up, held together by a nasty bracelet.

When the jail showed up I was just a bladder in pain. The entrance had been modelled on some ancient English castle. There were gentrifiers campaigning to keep it intact as the new Holloway prison was built. It was the only campaign about the conditions of the jail.

Papers were exchanged with the male screws on the main gate. "Come on, I'm bursting," I shouted. My personal screw was of the same opinion, he asked where the toilet was. A gate screw pointed in the general direction of some old buildings. The van drove into the yard, me and the screw jumped out and set off in a three-armed race and burst through a door. There was just the one toilet. His piss dragged on, was this what they called exquisite pain. So near but so far. As he finished I swung him on the cuffs to get in, let the bastard do his flies up outside. Oh, the pleasure, waves of it, on a par with the best of wanks.

We got our visit in a box either side of a heavy table bolted to the floor. Massive women in uniform stomped about. It was a miracle of relaxation talking at all. We didn't talk much of our daily lives, the screws could hear most of what we said and her conditions had always wound me up. They were much worse than ours, local nick conditions for long-term prisoners. I wanted to know about the parole thing. It seemed certain but she wanted to tell me about something else, the death of a prisoner. I'd read about it, she'd burned to death in Holloway's Observation wing. It was notorious and Hilary had been in another cell there the night it happened. She whispered to me how it had been. As the woman screamed, Hilary and other cons pressed their alarm bells. No response. They stayed on the bells. No response till the woman was dead. Then they'd been very busy.

I felt quiet all the way back to the mass of floodlights in the blackness. The lights of the antique shops in Chipping-this and Chipping-that left me cold.

It was like home being back on the wing but I just wanted the peace of the cell. I lay on the bed with my eyes closed and let the day soak in. Just being able to do it, the door open but without fear of interruption, it said a lot for the sensitivity of my friends there. It's a trusim, and it's true, that a jail can only work if the cons let it work, but there's another side to the story. There's that knowing how to live with other people in a small space, a necessary respect between cons that gave us the chance of coming out sane.

The next day, the day before Good Friday, I got hauled out of the VTC shop for a cell-spin. At the end of the search I refused to drop my strides and pants. Normally I'd drop them no problem, stride about the spur brazen, feeling my cock swinging and it would be the screws who'd cherry up. This time I just did not fancy it. Maybe it was the presence of Superscrew with his creepy uptight; maybe the smouldering from Hilary's account of life and death in the Observation wing.

I wound up down the block. No one gets weighed off on Good Friday, it's a day that gave the judicial process a bad name. A quiet lie-down over the Easter weekend, nothing better, just what I needed. Only then most of the Republican prisoners in the jail arrived. One of them had been fucked about over a Learning Gaelic book. As Joe had told me, the Brits had banned the language for hundreds of years and it seemed they couldn't get out of the habit. No chance of a quiet lie-down, not with all them and it being Easter as well. It was their big day, commemoration of the 1916 Rising and it would be commemorated in the L-L chokey same as anywhere else. Our faces close to the windows of our individual cells, texts were read out loud, songs sung. The Wee Man from the Falls Road, he sang a fighting song. Eddie, a lovely man off of another Wing he sang a lament. It was a long lament, verse after verse but Eddie had the voice for it, he cast a spell. Then Joe did another fighting song and it was my turn. I wasn't too hot at remembering the words of songs, didn't want to mug myself off and thought I had no chance of making it right through The Internationale. The only one I knew well was the Italian communist song Avanti Populo. It was in a language I didn't know but there weren't so many words and I did know those by heart. I gave it everything, so loud I could imagine the song breaking free of this inner sanctum, the jail within a jail. What an appreciative audience, invisible but appreciative. And Gerry took over, reciting a speech of James Connolly.

Back on the wing after Easter, me and Joe were starving from several days of enforced observance of the official diet, and the official diet only. The fact is we were a good foraging team. Not gannets, foragers. A gannet like Willie would make off with a whole tray of thin custard on cardboard pastry. We were

discriminating, paying minimal cash to cons in the kitchen for this and that, and paying the rest of the price by listening to their problems, hopes and bad luck. There was a Vietnamese guy from Wolverhampton who'd been caught up in some nationwide smack business. Half the time I just wanted to tell him that though I thought he was a great guy who'd done wonders for the standard of vegetable cooking in the kitchen, I did not want to hear about his innocence.

Fact was I thought smack to be a nasty business and even if I believed his innocence, there was fuck-all I could do about it. I said nothing of the sort — what I could do was listen, that was the price. This time I got caught up in the drama of his parole application and the complications involved in not letting his kids know where he was, his letters posted to Vietnam and then re-posted in fresh envelopes to Wolverhampton.

As well as these kitchen contacts, selective coups could be made off the hotplate itself. Weekend breakfasts which few of us got up for, they could be a good bet, a whole stash of marge of marmalade might be up for grabs.

The next Saturday morning I was woken up by Joe staggering about in my cell.

There was blood on the side of his head, plenty of it.

"He stabbed me the mad cunt."

"What? Who?"

"Gerry the cunt, he's stabbed me."

"What? Gerry?"

Gerry was a mate, that's why I was slow. But I looked again, saw the blood, that it was real, shot out of bed and pulled on my trousers.

"He's a nutter. What happens is, he's copped all the marmalade, I was just trying to get a bit of it, asking for a bit. For you, you bastard, so my old mate could have some marmalade," he said, ending with a grin.

That was good sign, nothing fatal.

"So what happened, you asked him for some of it..."

"And he stabbed me with some fucking scissors."

"Jesus wept, what he do that for."

"How the fuck do I know."

I got Joe to sit down and went down the recess for water. There was no buzz out on the spur. The aggravation had been in your man's cell on the Threes. It hadn't spilled out this far though I wasn't going up to the Threes to see how it was there. I bathed the side of Joe's head with a towel dipped in water.

It was a nasty cut. Maybe heal up without stitches. We had to give it a go.

Rizla were a good bet, I stuck two along the jagged.

"How's it feel?"

"What do you mean, how's it feel. Are you after a career in prison doctoring or something eh? You've got the damnfool questions right. It hurts like buggery is what it feels like."

"If I run now I could just make it to treatments for some Paracetemol or something."

"Go on then, I could use it."

"Any screws see you?"

"No."

"And your man's till in his cell."

"How the fuck do I know. Probably. Pigging down that fucking marmalade."

"OK, we'll give the Rizla a go, just don't touch them."

I ran off, shouted Headache to the screw at the wing gate and sprinted off through the corridors. At the weekends there was just a screw in his white jacket with a tray of pills and medicines. He was packing up as I arrived. I wheedled for the pills, did a head-clutching number and pretended to swallow them.

It was bad fucking business. Not like Harry's thing all those years ago in the Scrubs, I hadn't known the other guy then, and even then it had cost me. No, it was fucking bad. Maybe it was a very small world I lived in but this was like a big hole opening up in it. We'd all eaten together, had the crack, and Gerry, one of the few black cons in the jail, he'd been sound. I could be ratty in the mornings, raw and edgy from reentering prison for the umpteenth time, I could be ratty but I didn't start stabbing people.

Over the next few days news of the business filtered out. Larry was especially put out, he'd been spending a lot of time with Gerry. For me it was amazing how in such a tiny space as the wing I didn't see your man for days and when I did it had to be the blank. Joe was very quiet. I was sure he'd make a comeback but he only mentioned it the once and did not ask for help. Gerry knew the score, he'd have taken defensive measures for his cell. The reality of the situation hit me head-on a few days later. Walking down an a nearly empty corridor back to the wing, there was Gerry coming the other way. We could see each other thirty yards off. Thirty yards to put on and hold the blank. A bit of me wanted to burst out laughing. We passed each other our faces set, our bodies guarded and tense. Just a few days before we'd been talking of this and that right up to bang-up. Back on the wing I hoped Joe would make a comeback soon, not out of proportion but decisive all the same. It was the only way to take the poison out of the air.

I was learning overhead arc welds at the time and in the VTC shop only two things made me nervous: bits of molten metal dropping on my skull, and the random bangs on my booth, the Sailor getting his kicks out of whacking it with a hammer. It was those pheasants again, most every time I'd jump as the whack echoed round the booth.

"Give us a fucking break," I shouted.

The sailor popped his head round.

"Got a problem," he said, "see the Welfare. So what's the sp with young Joe, plotting up is he."

"I don't know, I'm his mate, not his fucking advisor."

"No need to get a cob on."

Back on the wing, things were quiet. I spent most of my time with Bob, a handsome African brummie who'd moved into the cell next to mine. I liked his seriousness broken up now and then by big laughs. And he wasn't involved in the aggravation, didn't even know about it. It was good, the last thing in the world I wanted was to talk about it, like it was all for our entertainment.

One evening after work I went down to Larry's cell at the far end of the Twos. I hadn't seen him much for a while. He'd been very low-key, didn't want to be middled up. We had a go at a few crossword clues still outstanding from the last fortnight's worth of The Times. We cracked a thirteen letter, 2 word affair, and wondered how the fuck it had taken so long, and a few four letter ones that felt like an achievment. When it was time for Tea I stepped out into the corridor. There was Gerry coming my way. It was blank at close-quarters in the narrow spur. He said All right in a near inaudible voice and I couldn't be sure if my head hadn't nodded a fraction in response. We passed by. I'd just stopped by the recess when I heard a quiet scream and there was Gerry hobbling in the corridor, cursing, blood spurting out of his thigh. He was raging but it was obvious, he was going to have to get it stitched which meant the screws knowing for a fact it had gone off. I knew Gerry wouldn't grass but the gossip would be enough, I'd seen it before, Joe would end up in the frame. The next evening Joe was shanghaied to another wing. He'd told me how he'd plotted up in Houdini's cell for four days because he knew Gerry some times called in there.

"He got a fucking shock when I jumped out, but then he knew I wasn't going to just leave it. If he's got any sense he'll call it quits now."

The day after Joe had gone I heard the first rumours that Gerry was after me.

"He thinks you set him up. He remembers seeing you at that end of the spur just before Joe done him."

Fucking brilliant, that was all I needed. I knew I hadn't set him up but that didn't make much difference. I thought it was all ridiculous but that didn't stop me getting hold of a broom handle. That night I wedged it behind the head of my bed and across the door. I had a lot of mates in the cells around me but I couldn't take chances, not with an early morning attack. The next day, the more gossip I heard, the more I thought I was getting dragged into a roundabout of paranoia that had no way of stopping. I didn't see the man himself at all. One moment I was sure I could sort it out, the next that this was wishful thinking on my part and that I'd had a gutful of wishful thinking. I couldn't see me using a blade either, but all the same, I made one on the grindstone in the workshop. I wasn't going down like an innocent and maybe I could force a stand-off. I told Larry the situation from my side: I didn't see how, looked out even from the outside, I could have set him up; but that I was on alert and well pissed off that I had to concentrate so much on it.

I was getting wound up enough to make a pre-emptive strike. This I did not tell Larry.

The impulse for a negotiated settlement came from a very different quarter. An ageing London face on the Twos was winding me up from outside. He kept telling me what a nutter Gerry was, and he knew that he was deadly serious about doing me. He went on and on about it. I was sure that he was both a racist and was looking for entertainment. In one moment, So what are you going to do about it John, I saw he was getting his rocks off at the prospect of a full-scale battle. I saw the nasty, manipulative bastard he was. Maybe Gerry had picked up those exact same vibes off the guy, or he'd just thought it out.

I was sat in my cell one lunchtime reading the paper when Gerry's head came cautiously round the door. I gave a start got my back to the wall. He opened his hands, showed they were empty.

"We've got to sort this out," he said. "I'll tell you straight I was in a rage and I thought you were in it with Joey. Now I'm sure you weren't. So can we cool it out."

I felt like saying all manner of things sarcastic, like what was it with marmalade and what, was I supposed to be grateful?

"OK, lets cool it out," I said. "The other way it's just too tiring. Yes OK, thanks for coming."

Not long after Joe was shanghaied to Wakefield. I was pissed off. It was a major loss, a loss for fuck all. I didn't see much of Gerry for a while and in the mornings, not at all.

FIRST THING

EIGHT FIFTEEN in the morning, the very last call for labour has already been made and two screws are going through the moves, the nudges and hints in the direction of getting a bloody move on to the workshops. We're supposed to be in the shops by ten past, but for a few of us on this spur, it's a struggle to make it for half past. It is anyway a very cold and dark morning. Waking up had been a battle through layers of sleep from a dream where I'd smelled the sea and felt the seaside sun in my eyes. I'd lain through ten minutes of dreading the mean cold in the cell, manufacturing, trying to manufacture some enthusiasm for the day. You know it's not that bad once you've got started and stuck into it, but that doesn't help much in getting there. And all the while I'd wanted a slash, felt the bladder nagging but would not move, stayed under the covers out of some perverse obstinacy. I stayed rigid in the pit to spite the bladder, to spite the scumbag going through the tannoy repertoire.

BREAKFAST. DOWNSTAIRS FOR BREAKFAST
LAST CALL FOR BREAKFAST
APPLICATIONS
TREATMENTS

WHEN I DID get out of bed it was for no reason, nothing had changed. It was more a perverse kind of willpower which had just happened. Then everything was on automatic pilot.

"All right Terry."

"All right John."

"OK Mick."

"All right mate."

"Larry, good to see you, how are you."

The p-and-t man gave me his barracuda grin.

"I feel fucking great," he said, daring me not to believe him. After a while, after using up all manner and modes of abuse, I'd learned not to question this statement. He moved off at speed, hair parallel to the ground.

The Sage has a much harder time and it is painful to be any part of the process of getting him up. I'd copped out of starting the process and as winter came on could not make it in time. My role now was simply to arrive at his cell at eight or five past with a big mug of nick tea heavily doused with sugar.

This morning I'd had to give that tea a hard sell to get any life out of him. He must have been up half the night painting. The cell stank of the stuff, a gothic canvas had taken on lashings of colour. I rushed off to my own cell to eat some porridge. It wasn't just guys like Gerry, the morning is a time to be on your own; a time when you don't want to think of anything or notice that even the Toots and the Maytals poster on the wall looks dull.

LAST CALL FOR LABOUR

LAST CALL FOR LABOUR

At ten-past I went back to the Sage's cell on back-up duty. He was out of bed and half-clothed. Most guys were on their way to work or had already long gone. Then I'd gone back to my own cell and crawled under the bed looking for my boots.

There was a tangle of odd-socks. I came out with the boots in my hand as a screw put his head round the door and said it was the last call for labour when I'd just heard it called on the tannoy. I put my boots on, stood up and saw him at the door again. Maybe he'd been there all the while. Either way he gave me a stare. It was a funny business this going to work. Dave the handball champ had been nicked a few weeks back for Persistent Lateness, but it was only him singled out and he's still usually late but they haven't nicked him again. It was something to do with the balance of forces in the jail, how far could they push on one thing or another without there being a comeback.

Eight fifteen in the morning. I move off back to the Sage's cell, thinking that at least we don't have to clock on like in Coldingley. His cell is in the wrong direction for the wing exit and the screw follows me. I meet the Sage in his doorway.

"Are you going to labour or not," the screw says. He is sullen.

I am not full of bravado, really not, but like most cons I'm at my most uptight in the morning.

"Why don't you get off my fucking back. I've got my boots on."

He backs off a little and marches up the landing. There might be a nicking in it there might not, but as I see it he'd be mugging himself off if he did, whatever the balance of forces.

We walk off down the landing and down the stairs to the wing exit. The corridors are empty.

"I was reading this report yesterday, it says violence on TV don't make people violent, it just makes them more nervous and passive."

The Sage grunts, I can just make out the word Obvious. He's my coach on the punchball and bag but he doesn't look well at all. Big black pits around his eyes. He looks fucking terrible. I don't say anything as we go out on the yards which is empty but for screws. We are the last of the stragglers, the bastards who are keeping them from their breakfasts. The Sage splits off to the laundry while the duty PO is hopping up and down in the middle of the yard, his walkie-talkie jabbering into his neck.

The working day of the VTC welding shop begins with the usual fifteen minutes in the khasi. The Sailor has his accustomed spot in Trap One and I have Trap Two. It's not a full sized crapper door, instead it has a two-tone gate that runs from ankle to stomach-height for the standing convict. The bright spark who dreamed it up had it in mind that the convict should have no opportunity to plot or conspire in the crapper. The mouthpiece in parliament said it reconciled security needs with the requirements of human dignity. Human Dignity, what does it require? I knew a guy in Brixton that couldn't shit at all in these conditions. OK, now and then I've had difficulty slashing in a crowded long urinal but for this guy it was torture. They gave him the whole range of laxatives, white stuff, blue, even the orange stuff that had the worst of reputations. For this guy it did nothing except make his intestines chime and bubble.

That's why Nixon called his Watergate hoods the plumbers. Yes, the plumbers, nipping down into the sewers and clearing the blockages to the system. Unsung heroes like those cop films where they make this kind of speech:—

"Yeah, we deal with all the problems and horrors the public don't want to see or know about. We have to go down in the shit everyday to clear up and what thanks to do we get. They call us pigs, that's the thanks we get. The DAs and the social workers throwing the rule book at us if we make the slightest infringement of the suspect's rights. Suspects rights, what the lawyers think is written in tablets of stone, the fucking lawyers who take home ten times what we do. And what do they do, they sit in offices like the Chief of Police and tell us what not to do because they don't know nothing because they never get out of their offices. Well fuck them."

That kind of speech in the films they show in the jail week in and week out.

And there it is for fucks sake, staring up at me from one of the old newspapers on the floor, a big picture with the barrel pointed straight at me. MAGNUM POWER RULES OK. Another movie advert. They nick everything these days, the wit, the slang, everything and now the graffitti slogan used to free George Davis, the arsehole. Nicked again. Above the advert there's a story about a vicar. I turn the page.

"I'm not up to doing much today," the Sailor says from the other side of the shoulder-high wall that divides Traps One and Two.

"I've done well just to get here."

"What are you whinging again!"

"Whinging, no I'm just telling you the score."

Milling machines and lathes rush into life. It's out there, the day, waiting. We've done basic engineering and now welding on this course, and the Sailor says he's worried. He's worried that he'll be sat in his local ale house and be talking Molecules and Reciprocals. Me, I just miss the gas welding now we're on the arc. With the gas it's mesmeric, get in tune with the slow speed of the molten pool that's neon green from behind the goggles, get in tune with that and you're away, as good as Dub.

"Mind you, sometimes I get in the booth, do a couple of welds and I'm well away," the Sailor says in a louder voice.

"Couldn't you make it more than sometimes and leave off hammering my booth. Middle-Aged Hooligan, that's what they'll have down in your record."

"I don't scare that easy and you're not taking my pleasures off me just like that. Besides you should be grateful, I'm just trying to help you stay awake in there."

"I could do with not being helped at all thanks all the

same."

"There you go again, what a terrible attitude you've got. That's what I tell Pete when you're pleading with him to cover up the cock-ups you've made."

"Yeah cock-ups that are due to you doing my nerves in."

"You're always dragging me in to it, you're getting bitter and twisted, it must be getting to you. I'm your pal, I'm there to help."

"I need your help like I need a…"

"You've enough holes in your head already, another one won't make any odds."

"Fuck me you're a bit quick off the mark for the time of day. What time is it anyway?"

"You're not at that already are you. You've only just got here. Sometimes I think me and the watch are just here for your benefit. The only reason you don't get one of your own is you'd get arm-ache looking at it every five minutes."

And he's talking about being bitter and twisted, I've only asked the cunt the time. I look down at the paper. There's another Vicar at it. Where do they find the time.

"Fucking hell there's an advert here for Gunfight at OK Corral," the Sailor says. "They're doing a re-run, makes me feel young again."

"Is that right."

"I wish I'd been around in those times."

"What times?"

"The Westerns, what do you think I'm talking about. I'd have gone around after the gunfighters, picked up the bullets and sold them for scrap."

"Now that really is small time. Just your bad luck they didn't have gas meters or phone boxes in those days, you'd have been in your element."

"Train robbery classy enough for you?"

"Yes, that would have been up to the mark."

"Yeah well, it was a fucking doddle in those days."

I see a guy hopping up and down in front of the crapper. I finish off with some super-thin, hard toilet paper which is unquestionably the property of HER MAJESTY'S GOVERNMENT.

THE ROAST

THIS TIME we were in my cell, seven of us, four on the bed and three on chairs. That's not bad for a tiny cube. Sometimes there's been nine and it's felt like one of those scenes where students break the world record for getting the greatest number of bodies in a phone box, the kind of story you get at the end of the news.

We're steaming into a pork hock, three in fact at 35p a throw. Fucking magic. No question but that part of me is straight carnivorous. It's the smell too, a roast joint is something else. In nick dinners the meat is cut into such thin slices that it hasn't the smell or the texture. There's not that much flesh on a hock but there's a pay-off in the flavour of the gravy and the way it's permeated the roast spuds in the oven.

I'd done the cooking with Larry, the p-and-t man, both of us a bit wrecked on a gram of Nepalese that we'd hung on to through the drought. We made a party of it with a radio down in the kitchen and the Alexis Korner Blues programme on at full blast. Screws kept coming out of the Wing Office to give us dirty looks and demanding the volume be turned down. We fiddled about with the volume dial and fended them off. As to the roast, after a few curses and panics we'd come up with the business.

I'd thought the smell of the dinner spreading through the wing would have pulled its co-investors in like a shot, but we had to drag them out of card games and the Sage out of his oil painting. There were sprouts, carrots and parsnip too and when I get round to serving it out I can hear Rashers explaining to my neighbour Bob what a trolley bus was and how it worked. A picture flashes up in my mind, one forgotten for fifteen odd years. I'm excited, bursting to spill it out. An opening comes.

"It was their acceleration man, it was something else, fast and smooth. I remember this time I'm on a bus, top deck of course, and it pulls in behind a trolley at some lights. So there's really fat kid in full school uniform can't resist it. He's off the bus and running for the trolley. Takes a jump, hand out to catch the rail, the lights turn green, the trolley's away whoosh, Bam, poor body lying all over the road."

"Laugh did you?" Jackie asks levelly. Jackie is a young, laid-back hooligan from the same part of the Black Country as Larry. He seems to be sleepy all the while and is a cheeky little sod.

"As it happens I did, a lot, loudly. It was the timing, as smooth as a well-rehearsed gag."

"You showed your true character at an early age," Jackie carries on, smug as you like, "that's why you're here today."

"OK wise-guy, what about all the other passengers, all they were was uptight because the body in the road is holding up the bus."

"A very understandable reaction, not like laughing."

"Reminds me of an experience on a commuter train, the no-corridor variety," the Sage says, dragging his face out of his plate. "The train was coming into the first big station as you come into London and I was in a compartment with a pin-striped and bowler hat sort of a man. So as the train slows down to stop, your man wakes up automatically, gets and up and marches out of the door. Next thing is the bowler hat and him underneath comes up again through the door, his faced all grazed and oily. He staggers through the compartment to the other side, the side with the platform. And he kept saying, Sorry, Terribly Sorry, that's when I started laughing."

"Malfunction on the automatic pilot," I said.

"So that's two of you with evil minds."

"Yes, they're the type," my neighbour Bob says. "I know you, you're the kind of bad guys who laugh when some old lady fall off her bike."

"No, not guilty, if I saw that happen I'd be sympathetic, helpful. It's the old-lady-falling-off-the-bike in the abstract that's funny," I said, sounding like a schoolmaster.

It was a funny sort of conversation altogether because anyone who wasn't talking was tuning into the bits of pork we'd managed to cut up with the bendy plastic knives which couldn't really cope with the reality of a joint of meat, however small and well-cooked. Everyone was eating with relaxed intensity, heads down. Larry was chewing one of the bones. This was not habitual, we couldn't afford it every week, and it wasn't pathetic, it was not one of those scenes where eyes dwelt enviously on the bone.

"To get back to commuters," I said, having to slow down to let my stomach expand," if you really want to suffer try the Bakerloo line at Oxford Circus during the rush hour. Make it a summer's afternoon, crushed against the door, elbows in your chest, feet aching. At the next stop you get a mouthful of musty air, but no one gets off. Why? Because it's Regents Park and nobody gets out at Regents Park. Then let the train get stuck in a tunnel."

"Must be very frustrating," Bob said coolly.

Having summoned up this picture of a less attractive feature of life outside I could see a pitfall. My obsession of the time was throwing out warning lights, I could almost hear brakes screeching, but like a wolly I let it all out.

"But give me the rush-hour any time, it's not going to last more than half an hour and after that, everything is open-ended. Have you heard all that cobblers about how we're all in our little prison, inside or out. Or, Never mind the bars, live in your head. Well I'm sick of living in my head. And memories, I've exhausted them. All that living-in-your-head stuff, it's just another christian pitch, there'll be pie in the sky by and by. Like singing We Shall Overcome Some Day. It's always Some Day and it sounds like a life sentence."

I stopped, exhausted.

"The lad can get really impassioned," Jackie said. "What you have said will be considered by the Board."

"The Home Secretary has considered your petition but regrets that he can find no reason...", the Sage said.

"Does he really say Regrets," Larry said. "He's got some front."

If you've got the power he has, you can be as outrageous as you like," Rashers said.

"Hey man," Bob said straight at me, "you always going on about you sick of memories, sick of the past, all that, but you always going on about the past."

I thought about it. I thought some more. Bob was right.

"You're right, I'm full of contradictions and ask for thirty similar offences to be taken into consideration."

"Thirty TICs," Jackie said, craning his head forward and moving his eyes like he's looking over the top of a judge's specs. "This is a very serious admission. Does the prisoner have anything to say in mitigation."

"Yes your honour, it's this place what does it."

"This court is sick and tired of defendants blaming their environment for their own wickedness."

Luckily he couldn't think of any more, I'd been steeling myself for a thousand year sentence.

"Look the real thing about tube trains is that they're bloody useless," the Sage said. "When you really need one after midnight, the fucking thing is closed."

I am a sucker for memories no two ways about it, and now he's set me off again. Nightime hitching back from the West

End to Cricklewood. I mentioned it to Rashers.

"There's one place you never hitch-hike," he said. "And you know where that is?"

We thought about it. We were getting nowhere.

"Belfast. You're walking home, maybe you've drunk a few," Rashers said and gave us a quick demo of swaying and staggering, "and a car pulls up to give you a lift, and you start running as fast as you can, ducking and weaving."

"I've never looked at Belfast that way."

"A great thing for sobering up."

"I wouldn't fancy hitching in the south of France either," Larry said, "not from what Jean-Pierre says."

"I can't see Jean-Pierre hitch-hiking," Jackie said.

"He was the driver you pudding. He gives a lift to this young bloke and the kid must have thought he'd got it made, a Porsche going all the way to Marseilles. Except they've only gone about 10 K when a cop car starts to flash them."

Our faces were lit up with expectation, even Gerry who'd been too busy eating to say anything at all.

"So Jean-Pierre puts his foot down even harder than it is already, leaves the flatfoots trailing. Another couple of K and there's a roadblock and when the kid sees Jean-Pierre's not slowing down, he really freaks."

Laughter was breaking out all over the cell. I could just picture the poor hitch-hiker, a few years back and it could have been me.

"Wham, they've swerved round the road-block, sirens are coming from behind and Jean-Pierre's asking the kid for his jacket. The guy's screaming to be let out and what does Jean-Pierre want his jacket for anyway. Jean-Pierre pulls out a shooter and lets off a couple of rounds, the car swerving all over the shop. The kid's pleading with him to slow down and let him out. They get clean away and when it's safe he slows down and does let him out, curses him for being unhelpful.

Then he asks him what the fuck he was freaking out for."

"A mite insensitive on his part," I said. Larry was at such a pitch he couldn't hold it any more, the punchline just rushed out. "The kid said, dead matter of fact, the same thing happened to me last month."

Tears ran down Bob's face but he managed to speak.

"You'd have thought the man learn his lesson."

"Hung up his thumb," Jackie said with a smirk.

"And whatever happened to twice-shy," Gerry said.

By the time the cell had subsided the meat was all gone, the bones were naked and only the smell remained. We were flush that week, we rolled and lit up cigarettes without the usual hassle.

"You know what I was reading in some magazine, there's people who believe Coronation Street is real, real people like, "Bob said. "They writes them letters, invite them to weddings, tell them their problems or they tell them what they should be doing."

"Don't get snotty about Coronation Street, just because I never miss it," Jackie said. "There's people think Sherlock Holmes was real, they go round to Baker Street and that."

"And Robin Hood," Larry said.

"Robin Hood," Rashers said, having been out of the game for a while trying to get some meat out of his teeth. "Now they say Robin Hood was a real person and in fact he was a big shot. A big shot who was done out of his land by another big shot. Which upset him so much he became an outlaw."

"They talk about him robbing the rich to give to the poor but I bet all the poor ever got was an arrow in the back a bit rapid."

We'd nearly finished our roll-ups when Kenny came in dressed in the shorts, boots and nick-shirt. He was holding a piece of paper. It was the next day's menu.

In Long Lartin they put up a scrawl to tell us what we'd be

eating the next day. In the Scrubs where the food had been worse, they'd only done that for Christmas Day and written the whole menu in Franch. There were more kicks reading it than the eating bit. I managed to describe all this, pommes this and haricot that.

"Nothing worse than being an ex-gourmet in the jail," Jackie said.

"How would you know."

I could see Kenny was getting impatient and I was trying to read the menu, trying to find out why he'd brought it, but the talk was out of control.

"It doesn't stop all thoe slags on The Sun telling the public we get better food for Christmas than the screws."

"They're so mean, it might be true."

I'd finally got to read the menu. Not bad, nothing special, only what was this, Kenny pointing to the bottom. Fucks sake, Melon. Melon. It's unheard of. Everyone else was too far gone into Christmas to be interested.

"All I remember about last Christmas," Gerry was saying, "is Willie with his Cheech and Chong record. He'd put it on but no one was laughing, only him. He must have noticed, so he kept saying, Just wait for the next one, that's a real cracker. So the next one comes and it's the same thing, his solo laugh. I was embarrassed for him."

I was mesmerized by the melon, it was taking on huge proportions in my mind. Kenny was gratified, and finally satisfied by my level of interest. He would leave it all in my good hands, he whispered, like we'd entered a conspiracy.

"What I like about this wing man, " Bob said, "is that come Christmas, they put the tree behind bars."

By now the melon had got too much for me, I muttered something about having to tell the Sailor and clambered out the cell. The Sailor was not at home. The spur was empty bar Phil the bookie who was tied up with his accounts, the racing page covered in figures and squiggles. I showed him the menu anyway, pointed to the melon. Interesting, he said, but that was it. I felt like Willie with his Christmas record. But fuck it, this was big news, I stayed eager and found the Sailor in the recess, brushing his teeth. I leant over from the next sink.

"Take a look at this," I said quietly, like it had become a conspiracy.

The Sailor was impressed, his eyes lit up and the toothbrush moved faster. I stood there waiting for him to finish. It was a lengthy business.

"Unprecedented," he said finally. "Tell you what, why don't you give me your slice."

"Fuck off."

"What a terrible attitude you've got."

I rushed off feeling like the geezer who took the good news from Aix to Ghent. I collared a lifer on the stairs. He didn't share my sense of marvel, it was obvious from his look. I had a flash of paranoia, supposing the big-shot in Ghent hadn't given a monkeys about the message. No fuck it, the lifer was just a deadhead. Down on the Ones it was the usual Saturday night desert, as if our cooking party had never happened. There were a few lost souls reading notices on the wing board. Odds on they were waiting for the very menu I had in my hand. My sense of marvel was fading fast, I felt empty and on the instant missed Joe badly. Fucking Gerry, sat up in my cell, he was all right. I stuck the menu back up on the board. The SO was sat in his office with the screws. Two cons were now reading the menu, they showed no excitement. Out of frustration or nostalgia for Joe, I manouevred the two of them between me and the office, and slammed my elbow into the alarm bell. On the stairs up to the Twos I heard the thunder of screws' boots and the wing door crashing open. I pulled open my cell door and the fragrance of roast meat and Old H hit me afresh. Larry and the Sage were in the middle of an argument. The vibes were intense, they were humming.

"You're avoiding the question of sex-cases. What are you going to do with them. I've got kids, " Larry was saying.

"People's justice doesn't need prisons to deal with sex-cases," the Sage said, his head moving closer to the p-and-t man across the table.

"What, so it's instant knee-capping is it, and you think that's more advanced than imprisonment?"

Everyone else was quiet but Gerry was getting restless, it was obvious.

"And you're going to tell me how wonderful prison is I suppose," the Sage said. "Twisted minds in their cells, their fantasies growing unchecked every night. What does prison do for anyone? The Establishment, they don't even talk re-habilitation any more."

"So a lot of them can never be let out."

"Oh very civilized."

Gerry'd had enough, he let rip.

"Quit stalling the both of you, don't talk about other people, should you two be inside."

Larry was shocked. He sat back in his chair.

"Me, of course not, I was doing a public service. It was good black I was moving not fucking smack. Bringing a good product from producer to consumer."

The Sage was less animated.

"I'm a prisoner of war in a foreign country. When we've won that war and our freedom, they won't have the power to imprison me and I wouldn't have to fight them."

Larry was still outraged.

"And I'm not a nonce either. So what do you think John, I've never known you keep your trap shut for so long. Can you see a society without jails."

"One thing I do know is that in any civilized society no one should have to be a screw, and no one should be allowed to be one."

"You're stalling, that means no jails."

"Not necessarily."

"But all the people you might have to put away, if there were no screws they'd end up killing each other."

"That would be their problem, besides what could be better as a fucking deterrent. And it's secondary to the fact that no one should be opened to the self-brutalisation that being a screw entails."

"The man's got a point there," Bob said.

The cell door opened to a powerful stink of unripe hooch followed by Phil the bookie. He looked at me and the sage, eyebrows raised.

"Sorry gents, looks like our manufacturing concern has gone into liquidation."

Oh.

Oh no.

Me and the Sage we shot up and out of the door. What a stink, it was brewery strength. Out on the spur Phil grabbed my arm.

"No point in rushing, it's beyond salvage."

We edged towards the recess, the smell getting stronger. Jesus wept, it was running down the fucking walls, a puddle spread on the recess floor. The guards sat outside the TV room were smirking, big smirks on their chops. I was mesmerised by the clock on the recess wall, the hooch seeping round its perimeter, dribbling down its face. We walked on past the recess and down the far spur.

"What the fuck happened?"

"Can only be two things, either the bucket tipped over, tilted off the ceiling beams, that or it was fermenting so strong it overflowed."

It was a sickener, a kick in the bollocks. For ten days we'd lovingly fed it sugar every day. A concoction of oranges and rice, it was going to be a cracker. We'd planned to filter it in two days time and then leave it to settle as long as our self-control lasted, a week maybe, as much as that. I'd felt so confident, the stash was brilliant.

"How much sugar did you put in John?"

"Two spoonfuls, same as before."

"Put it down to experience," the Sage said.

"No good crying over split hooch," Phil said. "Can't have the guards seeing us miserable."

I was miserable. I'd had expectations, I'd made an effort. The recess was full of sightseers from the TV room. The wall clock was dripping. Fucking thing. The least could happen was that the lost hooch would fuck up its mechanism but no, there were its hands, still ticking away.

Me and the Sage walked back like we were doing auditions for the role of stoic. The cell was in full swing. Larry was rolling the perfect spliff and Rashers had the floor.

"A very dangerous man that Robert Mark. He has a few of the really bent peelers lifted which impressed your liberal people. They don't want that kind of corruption for money anyway."

As it happened Rashers was the one other person in the cell with a direct interest in the hooch. We told him what had happened, only he just looked at us like we were delinquent kids and carried on with what he was saying.

"You take my point, that gave him the room to strengthen their power and their propaganda."

"But he didn't touch the fit-up cops," Bob said, anger in his voice.

Gerry had stirred from his normal comatose position.

"Did I tell you about this book a Chief Constable has written. He says you should watch out for joggers."

"I thought jogging was the business these days, beyond reproach," I said. "Every time I open a Sunday paper there's a picture of some grinning loony in a tracksuit who happens to be a bank manager who saw the light and discovered jogging."

"That's because they found out they were going down like flies, with coronaries."

"It's all bollox," I said. "It's mostly down to diet and you've got to have a few bob for a decent diet."

"The communists, always on their soapbox," Jackie said.

"As it happens I read something from a Chief Constable. Maybe it's the same one. If it is then he's really got it in for joggers."

"But how can he," Larry said. "It's so respectable, they advertise it on telly."

"If it's on telly why bother to go out and do it, you can sit in comfort and watch it," the Sage said, refusing the spliff and passing it to me.

"I wonder if the Health Council or whoever it is puts out these adverts, I wonder if they know there are people like you around," I said and took a stiff toke on the spliff.

"They know far too much about me already."

"Just in case you're interested I was in the middle of saying something," Jackie said evenly.

"Don't give us any injured dignity bollox, fucks sake."

"Or any false modesty. That's bad shit, like when Larry starts off saying No Disrespect and then tells you what an arsehole you are," I said, and passed the spliff on to Gerry.

Rashers had just started to say he was glad fitness had never appealed to him because it seemed like a risky business when Jackie shouted out loud, "Especially for joggers because this top cop also says jogging may well be a cover for casing houses."

"I could think of easier ways."

"He tops it off by saying you should also have your eyes peeled for anyone coming out of a public toilet with a damp sleeve," Jackie said. "It means they've been stashing contraband in the cistern."

Gerry's laugh started slow and loud. It got louder, He spoke in gasps. "I can see it now, a revolution in police techniques. A revolution."

He was clutching his stomach, struggling to speak.

"Instead of feeling your collar, they'll, they'll feel your sleeve."

Once he'd got the words out, the floodgates opened, tears ran down his cheeks as he slammed the table with his fist. Laughter is infectious stuff, only Larry and Rashers were immune, they looked at us po-faced like we were nutters. As soon as it had died down a little, Larry stepped in briskly.

"After all these evenings here I've got the feeling that there's a great big conspiracy out there to insult our intelligence, the adverts, the telly, the papers..."

"And books," Jackie said. "That copper's one is selling at seven quid a time."

"They're shameless."

"Arrogant more like it," I said. "They want to make out that most everyone is stupid to justify the specialisation of power. If they don't do that, then their own credentials don't stand up to the glare. It's like having a moody passport, when you're not sure, think it won't pass muster then you'll behave in exactly the way that will bring close scrutiny."

"They're just persistent man," Bob said. "There's so much lie every day, in the end you just give up."

"Anyone got any matches?"

There were no matches anywhere as it turned out but we looked just the same. Contrary to experience I always believe there must be papers and matches around somewhere, worse I look in the same places several times. There were no matches.

"More to the point, I'm going to let off a terrific fart any moment," Larry said.

"Why are you telling us man?" Gerry asked evenly.

"I thought I'd do you a favour by telling you in advance."

"And I suppose you'd like us to thank you for the privilege," Gerry said, serious and mean.

"Well I'm off for some matches," Jackie said. He was propelled across three pairs of knees and the heavy door was swung open for him. He was unruffled but looked both ways from the doorway like he was stepping into alien territory. It allowed some fresher air into the cell and encouraged Larry to stick his bum out of the door and let go. Rashers looked pained by the whole business, like we were juveniles again.

"The thing about Robert Mark and the liberals is that he pulled it off because they've got this blind spot," he said.

"And just what do you mean by that," Larry said, back in the cell, "being a liberal sort of person myself."

"Not like you," Rashers said with that pained look. "I mean the ones who read the expensive Sunday papers, the ones who think that if someone is brainy and has a way with words, then he must be liberal, humane and all the rest."

"What, they can't or won't believe there are clever reactionary bastards."

"Something like that. His campaign against peelers who were corrupt for money, well it made it easy for the other sort, the ones who do the fit ups. It's a terrible thing, the way they get away with their verbals."

I knew about Rashers' verbals, long after his trial he'd found them word for word in a Leslie Thomas book. He went on and on about his verbals, and if I'd found mine in a book, I'd have done the same.

"The worst I ever heard was what they stuck on my mate Eddie in the Scrubs. They nicked him on a ready-eye and as if that wasn't enough, they verbal him too. When it's come on top they have down as saying Kill The Pigs, like he's in a movie."

Jackie came back in, was asked if he'd got any matches.

"Didn't interrupt did I, it sounds serious enough to have been political."

"Never mind that you coy fucker, where's the matches."

"A con who shall remain nameless told me I was a ponce. A ponce, I said, you must have got the wrong man, I'm a socialist. That shut him up."

"You're really dragging this aren't you, you little toe-rag," Gerry said in his level voice.

"A big toe please."

"And a try-and-be-witty fucker to boot. That can be a big mistake Jackie, like in police stations, like here and now if you don't come across with those matches."

I noticed just how soggy my unlit roll-up had become in my mouth.

"Have a light for fucks sake," Jackie said. "I'm not likely to be in a cop shop for a while yet."

Larry was shouting, animated.

"We were talking about verbals and just for once I have something to say."

"Very sorry I'm sure sorr," Rashers said, feigning a touch of the forelock on his bald head.

"They operate off formula, you know what I mean. You express bravado and at the same time admit your guilt."

"Of course I done it but you'll never be able to prove it, that kind of thing," Bob said.

"Exactly, or in my case, That bastard must have grassed me up, I'll kill him. Now what kind of idiot is going to say that?"

"Sometimes there's a balls up, like that geordie in B wing, all his verbals were cockney," I said.

"What happened to him?"

"Wound up with a six stretch."

"Just shows you what mugs juries are," Gerry said.

"Bollox. Why do you think they're trying to get rid of

them. OK, if you're somewhere like Winchester you'll get a bunch of fascists but at the Bailey you can get a result. There's a fair chance some of the jurors will have experienced the filth first-hand."

The tannoy was crackling. It crackled some more.

GREEN TO THE OFFICE

GREEN TO THE OFFICE

It was Jackie.

"Private session with the SO son?"

"Parole preliminaries Jackie? Tell them your life story, how you never stood a chance."

"It just so happens," he said with a sleepy, sarcastic dignity. "that I'm not even down for parole now."

"Shame, shame."

"And furthermore," Jackie started to say like he was going to line up a wisecrack.

"Furthermore you'll be in wig and gown soon, the way you're going," the Sage said, his voice overloaded with sarcasm. "Will you remember your old pals then?"

"Furthermore toerag they can keep on shouting on that tannoy as far as I'm concerned."

"Do you realise this little fucker still hasn't come up with those matches," Gerry said.

It was true. How had it happened? My roll-up was sopping in my mouth.

"No, no not at all, I'd just forgotten about them, and you did as well," Jackie said. He struggled to his feet, made a big deal out of getting the matches out of his pocket. He finally succeeded to undeserved applause. We lit up, it was a big hassle getting a draw on my fag. It had got black dark outside, the perimeter floodlights had come on

"They keep talking about new rules on verbals but they'll never get rid of them, they depend on them," Rashers said.

"Conspiracy and verbals, they couldn't do without them."

"And grasses," Bob said. "They don't do any of that patient detective work them talk about."

"Sure, detection was never the name of the game, you can leave that to your man Sherlock Holmes."

"All Sherlock Holmes would get is a pull for cocaine possession and if he couldn't settle it with a backhander, his experience of detection would have been on the end of some right-handers in West End Central."

"They'd love a wise-guy like him that was always mugging them off, the flatfoots. They'd have bumped up the possession rap with an Intent To Supply."

"Dr Watson grassed him up," I said. "He was always trying to get him to kick the habit."

"You know what they do in Israel or some place like that," Bob said. "They bump them off and leave the body outside one of those monastery places, you know where they're not allowed to talk."

"Trappists. Stylish. You sure they don't cut their tongues out as well?"

"That would be over the top," Larry said, "laying it on a bit thick."

"I'll tell you who does lay it on a bit thick, your man who does the Great Trials programme on the radio," the Sage said.

"Edgar Lustgarten."

"Aye, him. Him with the ham acting. He thought he was Mastermind till the noose touched his neck."

"What on a coke possession rap, that's a bit heavy. Didn't they have Appeals then," Jackie said. What was it with him this evening? He'd been remorseless.

GREEN TO THE OFFICE
GREEN TO THE OFFICE.

That slowed him down, and the Sage took his opportunity in a weary voice.

"Do us a favour and see what the crack is or we'll have this all night."

"It goes against the grain."

"Think of your friends," Bob said.

Jackie got up from his spot on the bed like it was an exhausting business. When we'd helped him out the door, the Sage said he was going to get back to where he was.

"The whole style of that fucking programme is Arrogance gets its just desserts, Is Mastermind chuckling now, that kind of thing. It's all done to prop up the ego of your average sort of person."

"What, and meanwhile they're constantly deceiving and abusing that same average person?"

"That's the problem," the Sage said, "it's like with verbals again, we know it's all bullshit but your man in the street, he believes the Peelers every time. Or they believe some mumbo-jumbo about the national interest."

"Bollox," I said. "People aren't conned, they know that pulling up their socks and tightening their belts isn't going to do them any good. They know that?"

"So what do they see?"

"They see plenty of things, but not the possibility that they'd win any decisive showdown with the ruling class. And if everyone believed what they read in the papers, the country would be to the right of Ghengis Khan."

"You're being naive, a crazy optimist."

"Am I? As it happens we were talking about juries. Are you going to tell me you'd prefer a judge on his tod, some special court?"

"But we're still in here all the same and they told some terrible lies in my case, " Rashers said.

"They'd believe anything, the mugs," Gerry said.

"So why are there so many acquittals in London courts? Why was that same bastard Robert Mark mouthing off against them. Right in the middle of my trial he made a speech saying juries had a duty to believe the rozzers whatever, and if they failed to do so, they should be abolished."

"He's got a point," Bob said. "You wouldn't see me in front of a magistrate if I could get a jury trial."

"All right, they're slightly better," Gerry said like it was being wrenched out of him.

"It's the one time in this fucking country where a group of ordinary people have real power, the power to make decisions with consequences. To the degree we've got a free society at all it's down to juries, not bloody parliament."

"We all know parliament's a joke,"! Larry said, "but the mugs still go out and vote."

"Like it's a fucking privilege to choose between one set of public school monkeys and another every five years,"

Gerry shouted. "I keep hearing how criminals are all Tories but show me a serious criminal who's ever fucking voted and I'll give you my melon ration tomorrow."

"How do you know about that melon," I asked. I was frowning. Gerry hadn't seen the menu.

"Sources close to the kitchen, " he said blandly.

"What melon, what is this?"

"It's on the menu for tomorrow, it's what Kenny came in to tell us."

"When?"

"When we were eating, I was trying to tell you but you were all busy with something."

"Melon? You're kidding."

"I'll take you up on that bet," Larry said, his voice eager.

"What bet?"

"Quit stalling Gerry, a slice of melon for a voting criminal, that's what you said."

"Who are you going to ask?"

"I'm not telling you, you'd nobble him."

"Me?"

Gerry's innocence was stagey, he was uneasy and Bob latched on to it.

"Be a man and put your stomach where your mouth is man."

"All right, but no nonces."

Larry fairly flew out of the cell, he was on to something, it was obvious, some one as a sure thing. Gerry looked shaken. I'd never seen him like this before, a poker-faced Kalooki whizz looking rattled. He changed tack.

"What I'm saying is this, it's only us thieves who really tell them to fuck off. I'm not pulling my belt in for the national interest."

The door crashed open with Larry. He was shouting.

"Mr Big, once voted Labour, thinks it was 1959."

"A youthful indiscretion," Gerry said, visibly shaken that it was his number one Kalooki rival who'd been the weak point.

"That slice of melon is going to be even more temporary," Larry said and licked his moustache. "By the way there's a terrible smell out there, a very young wine I'd say."

"Thanks pal," I said.

"All right, all right," Gerry said, but none of this alters the fact that it's us thieves who don't take their bullshit. They're telling me to be satisfied with my lot, be a mug, accept that I can't have their kind of dough, their kind of lifestyle."

"But not everyone can be a thief," I said.

"Yeah, the rich don't need to and most of the others get their bottle knocked out of them early on."

"OK, maybe that's true but objectively everyone can't be a thief because then there'd be no one producing anything and there'd be nothing there to thieve."

"So you're saying I should eat shit just because everyone doesn't avoid eating shit."

"I'm saying that what's turned me on the most is when I've been part of a lot of people together saying they're not going to eat a particular piece of shit, and then act on it. When they do, the whole mountain of shit comes into question."

"Well it's never happened to me," Gerry said. "I worked straight for eighteen months of my life and I resent every minute of it. The union never did fuck all."

"It's happened to me," Rashers said, "but not with the union. It happens in Ireland, most of the people of West Belfast who know the law is only there to keep them down, they're not afraid to break it. That's why the Brits hate us, that's why there's an army of occupation. The unions here are all scared of the law."

"Not in 1972. I was at that Saltley man," Bob said. "I never seen so many police going down."

"That was a one-off," Rashers said, "they'll still be jawing about that in 2000AD. What's here and now is my case. Thirty years I'm in the Transport and General, paid my subs, unionized whole shops. So I write to Jack Jones about my verbals and what do I get, not even a reply."

"Just what I'm saying, don't trust those cunts whatever they say they are," Gerry said. "Go out and make your own dough. As soon as someone starts doing things for the good of all, you can bet he's going to do well out of telling you what the good is."

The door tried to burst open and Jackie more or less fell in. "You're not going to believe this..."

"But?"

"That SO, he's just like my auntie, said I wasn't looking well and the doctor wanted to see me on Monday morning. My name shouted all over the wing just for a doctor's call up."

"You look all right to me."

"No, he looks terrible."

"Hey, I don't want to be personal," Gerry said in Larry's direction, his voice deceptively sleepy, "but when did you last change your socks."

I hadn't noticed it till then but the cell had lost its cafe smell, instead it stank, it was fucking humming and there was Larry sat there with his shoes off. He gave his socks a baleful look and said, Yesterday, yesterday he'd changed them.

"Who with, " Jackie said.

"Jesus you're quick tonight," Larry said generously. "So quick you could just steam through the washing up which you haven't done for weeks."

"I'm terrible at washing up."

"Too bad, there's no better time to learn and no better man to teach you," the Sage said in a brisk PTI's voice.

"How can anyone be bad at washing-up?"

"You haven't seen me yet."

"We don't want to see you, we want you to fuck off and do it," Larry said, helpfully piling plates, plastics and pans into his arms.

I must have gone off into a day dream, some memory of me and Julian doing the washing up in the Scrubs for Table Nine, picturing it and the Table Nine gang.

"Washing up's not such a big deal," I said.

"What are you talking about man," Gerry said. "I'm saying you've got to make your own dough and your own freedom before you get involved in everyone else's. We're saying most of them don't even want it, if they didn't have their mortgages and pensions and TVs, they'd freak out. That's what we're talking about and all you can talk about is washing up."

"I just don't think that making your money necessarily gives you that freedom. Even with your dough it's still only the same old shit to consume."

"What are you trying to tell me there's no difference between beans on toast and a good french dinner?"

"Don't try and ring it, I never said anything like it."

"Well what the fuck are you saying then?"

"I'm saying everyone should be able to eat well, and just

because you're rich doesn't change the totality of what's on offer. I'm also saying it's not just thieves who reject all their crap."

"Yeah but we don't just reject it, we act on it."

END OF ASSOCIATION

END OF ASSOCIATION

Shit, another rush job it was going to be. I scrambled out on to the spur with Larry. He pointed out a news screw walking up and down.

"See that plum there, he's ambitious and stupid. You know what he says to Houdini, tells him to let him know if he Hears Anything. Yes, and drops lead weight hints to me about contraband."

In the recess the smell of hooch lingered but they'd obviously had a cleaner on the job, the puddle was gone. What a fucking waste. Maybe the cleaner had got pissed on the fumes but that was it, a fucking waste. I had not put too much sugar in, the bucket had looked solid on the joists. Fucking thing had a life of its own.

I went over to the sinks where Jackie was on the job.

"If anyone ever tells you again that you can't wash up, just send them to me, I'll put them straight."

"This is first class work," Larry said. "We might be able to make this into a permanent post.

"It already is," Jackie said, walking across to the urinals. Pissing next to him was a London face in immaculately laundered clothes. Jackie was staring studiously at the ceiling. Suddenly he rushed off leaving the London face looking aghast, finding whatever it was, hard to credit.

I had to go to Jackie's cell for an eighth of Old H. What had happened?

"I was so intent on avoiding his terrible conversation," Jackie said, "that I didn't look properly, I was pissing down his trousers for some time."

Time Up

MY CELL had been notorious. Old newspapers spilled out from their stash under the bed. The Harrier had brought faces from other wings to look at it. Now it was empty, the bins on the landing were full of these same old papers and I'd already given the striped rug and, record player and radio to the Sage and handed out my books and letters. The cell was as bare as my first one in Brixton, the very emptiness gave me a sense of freedom.

As it was, the Harrier was the guy who'd given me the first taste of the experience when he came back from a Home Leave. His whole face had been lit-up. Having me down as an out-and-out druggie and scruff, he said his couple of days had been how he imagined an acid trip to be.

"Not acid, mushrooms, " I said. "Synthetic chemicals have got a bad name these days and mushrooms are free."

You've always got to get your 5p's worth haven't you, can't resist it. Anyway, how do you know."

"I have visits, get an idea of what's going on in the world."

"Visits? Second-hand John, there's nothing like the real thing."

Everything had been in sharp technicolour, he said, every second a pleasure and discovery. "I must have had a big grin on my face all the time, and every time I saw a drawn, tense face I just wanted to say, Don't be ridiculous, what a waste of life, you only live once."

"I bet just seeing your face gave some of those people a lift."

"Bollox, if they noticed me at all they'd be saying, who's this flash cunt, what's he so pleased about."

"Well stick to the people who do get a buzz off of your cheerfulness."

"Yeah man, OK man," he said before taking another delighted bite of his sausage sandwich. He'd been on a vegetarian diet for 8 stretch and then decided a couple of day after the Home Leave that he didn't need the abstinence any more. He retained only an ambition, to live to be a hundred, get a telegram off the queen or king, and write back telling them to stuff it.

"I just hope it lasts," he said, "that sharp feeling, that delight. I don't want it getting ground down."

"Yes this friend of mine on a visit the other week she said she envied me for the going-out feeling I'll get."

"You tell her that seven stretch is a big investment for such a moment."

At this point I had four months left to do. I'd never put in for parole but I had put in for a weekend Home Leave. I got a blank and decided it was all for the good. Despite the Harrier's delight, other people had said that doing the bird afterwards was double murder and giving yourself up again, reporting back to the prison, it sounded very much against the grain. It didn't stop me applying for Terminal Home Leave, a weekend soon before final release, the temptation was too much though it seemed perverse that I should see it like that. Yes, I wanted it. I wanted some freedom immediately and there was a bit of me getting nervous about this final freedom, the final release, how about some preparation.

A month later I got a knock-back on that too while the Harrier got a few months unexpected parole. For both of us the life of the nick was losing importance. All the battles and conflicts, the news, the gossip, it all felt removed.

"We forget what a little pool this is. It's too easy to feel important here. Anyway I'm not going to get back into a little pool on the out, no more drinking clubs and villains' pubs for me. It's a big world out there and I'm going to make the most of it."

The Harrier's going was a loss but inspiring too. Sentences did come to an end, a friend had actually walked out of the gate. It had happened before but not with the edge it had now I was close myself. I remembered those paranoias of 1974 when there was talk of military coups and I'd feared some internment scenario over here, when release would just be a matter of gate-arrest and back inside without a date.

When I had six weeks to go, I discovered it was seven. I'd got my EDR wrong, forgotten a particular week's loss of remission. A farce that had been. I'd gone in to the TV room because they were showing Cool Hand Luke. It had just got to that great bit where he's escaped and is sending pictures and cards back to the nick showing what a great time he's having even when he's not. Bosh, the TV went off, ten to nine, switched off by some remote control from the Wing Office. It was a film must have gone straight to the heart, we were pissed off, refused to budge till they put it back on again. The minutes went by and we knew we weren't going to see it anyway but a few of us felt obstinate, sat there till the time the film would have finished. The Governor'd thought it was worth a week's remission and I'd forgotten it.

Still the screws who ran the wing gave the appearance of feeling that the the KB on the Home Leave was a bit over the top; it was they who'd had to give the news. So I got a cleaners job doing the corridors with Attilla. It was a doddle which we got down to half an hour a day with the creation of the Super-Mop, three mop-heads on one handle. I spent most of my time on the wing indulging myself with some red leb and dub albums of Joe Gibbs and King Tubby. On the strength of the screws embarrassment I also pushed for extra vists via the welfare. It was the first time I'd ever had any dealings with them and I screwed plenty of visits out of them.

Visits were a time for dressing-up. A pal in the laundry would press my hand-made strides and the prison shirt with a re-tailored collar. A good feeling the dressing up but I always got a bit tense when it was time for the visit; would they come;

then the hoops, going through all the gates and rub-downs to get there, trying to remember all the things I wanted to say. Sometimes I couldn't get out of a self-defeating mania; sometimes I'd get the hump if my visitors didn't share my sense of urgency about one thing or the other. Sometimes it would be perfect, relaxed and easy; then I'd listen to the realities and joys of everyday life that made my urgencies a bit ridiculous. Over the years new realities became clear. Like friends who were lovers having their own separate places to live, a rediscovery of the need for privacy. After years of a single cell, it made sense to me. In other ways changes in how I saw the world seemed to be going in step with my friends. When that became clear, in a single sentence or over the whole visit, we'd be pleasantly surprised and then not surprised; after all we were living through the same times. Mostly it was a matter of recognising in what a ghetto revolutionary politics existed. Only when that recognition resulted in friends joining the Labour or Communist parties did I get the hump. It seemed like a desperate substitute or a short cut into a larger, managerial ghetto. More exciting was the way squatting had become a mass movement in London. The possibility of undermining the perverted relations of property without and outside of institutions, and of the comforting revolutionary ghetto, without preaching or recruiting, was inspiring. And I needed some inspiration because it had seemed for two years and more that I was going out into a period of defeat.

My last visit was four days before release. It was Hilary and I didn't feel tense at all. Since her parole, every visit like this had been a bonus after the cramped, screw-crowded inter-prison visits we'd had.

"Here I am," I said, "hermetically sealed in the middle of nowhere, Worcestershire, I'll have no resistance. There'll be germs lining up to have a pop at me. Here look at this mug, no defences, what a pushover."

"We'll look after you," she said laughing and the warmth of our intimacy came alive until the Visiting room full of screws, kids and WVS ladies with the tea, didn't exist any more. Only that we didn't make love there and then, just touching hands and kissing I felt my cock go stiff. It still didn't seem real that in a few days we'd be on our own together with no limits. Part of me wondered if I'd be instinctively looking for limits, if I might be a textbook case of the fear of freedom, but my cock was warm and glowing.

It was right at the end that she told me her Parole Officer had banned her from meeting me at the gates and insisted she pay a visit to the house on the day of my release. Fear of publicity was her reason. There's no accounting for some people's paranoias, we'd come out of the swinging sixties and now was the severe late-seventies, I couldn't see the press being interested. I felt a quick rage, here was another officious scumbag making herself busy.

Talking to Kenny the next day he said I'd done my bird well, would be going out in pretty good shape, not too many scars.

"I'm not sure about that. We can understand conditioning, understand such a process exists, even the hows and whys, but that don't mean it hasn't happened to us."

"What, and there's no people on the out conditioned. All I'm saying, though now I don't know why I bothered, is that you haven't done too bad on that score, not too many lines on the face."

"That's just front," I said laughing. Because I didn't know, didn't know yet what it had done to me, wouldn't know for a long while. "But thanks for saying it, if I need a testimonial, I'll call you. Anyway, what's it like if you haven't done it well."

"You go out cowed, bitter and twisted," Kenny said, like he'd thought about it.

On my last night Liverpool were in the European Cup

Final. Any other time, even it was Liverpool, it would have been the highlight of the week. This time it just meant the exercise field was close to empty. It was a fine evening and I made a conscious effort to put the scene on my head-film so I'd never forget. Another mate had told me how quickly you forget it. I didn't want that to happen. For one thing remembering might be necessary to hold on to that feeling of fresh delight the Harrier had described.

A friend caught up with me and put a small piece of dope in my hand. To be smoked the next morning he said, a small celebration. Good timing, I hadn't got a crumb left. Back on the wing I knocked off a little bit for Larry who'd finally given up pin-and-thread and looked all the better for it. We looked in on the TV room but I couldn't relate to it. The excitement was breaking out all over me, in comparison, the excitement of the televised crowd seemed very thin stuff.

We went back to his cell and rolled a single-skinner, which still left me a piece for the morning. Suddenly there was a rushing of feet. The game was over and I had to get myself together to say a raft of goodbyes in a few minutes.

I shook hands.

"Be lucky John."

It was all a blur. Then into the Sage's cell and something else hit me. It was all so familiar. The easel up in the cell, paints all over the place, the jug of tea, the smell of pipe tobacco. My good friend had at least another eight stretch. We embraced, tears in my eyes for the first time in four years.

Then bang, my door was shut. I'd done it. Done it. UP YOURS.

I sat cross-legged on the bed, my back to the wall and rubbed my hand up its slight roughness. This was real. Then some anxious feelings wormed in. Cons I'd seen released saying, You'll never see me here again; I'd seen some of them. A hole opened up, more stuff crept through. I hoped the cops weren't going to be on my back. It was a depressed world I was going into, it had all gone the other way since 1975 finalised by the defeat in Portugal. Now my optimism, me Dave and Irish Gerry, it all seemed naive, not weighing the rhetoric of conscript soldiers against the unthinking experience of the regular troops there. But the defeat hurt, it was far away but made our hopes that bit weaker. All over the world the ruling classes had got away with blaming what they called an economic crisis on the workers and peasants of the world, had even used a momentary concern with the finiteness of natural resources to this end. Then they'd started to make them pay. They were shameless, brazen. They were selfish bastards and they ruled the world.

I remembered the escape project too, a fragile possibility but possible, my desire for it half-based on crazy expectations that capitalism in Britain, its control and discipline could not hold together, that things were falling apart and everything was up for grabs. Wild optimism and then a few weeks later, Els was dead. And who knew? Maybe if I'd been there Ian wouldn't have fallen off the ladder and we'd have made it. And who knew, if I'd made it, maybe Els would not have gone to Holland, not got the viruses. Not died. And instead? I knew now why I'd been shanghaied, it had had hit me as a KO in the very same TV room, F Wing Long Lartin. A documentary about the Scrubs, one of those that bombards you with in-depth analysis as a substitute for change. There suddenly had been the face of the D Wing AG, how he'd once had to break up a dangerous mixture of anarchists and psychopaths.

"Lying shit," I'd been shouting at the TV screen.

"What's he raving on about now," Jackie'd said.

"Raving? Raving? That fucker up there, I know him and he's lying."

Saying it because the penny had dropped, that it had been Harry's over the top revenge that had led to the spate of shanghais and how I'd gone along with it. Not been a serious person.

But this is victory day Johnny, don't bring yourself down, not now for fucks sake. You've survived, you've won. Hypocrite, how many times have you said that people have got to learn to celebrate and use their victories. Victory, don't you fucking understand, you've had them over, you're going out and it's going to be great.

I wanted to sleep and I didn't want to sleep; wanted it to be tomorrow and to revel in this last night. I wrote two notes, a comic one to Larry, emotional to the Sage. I pressed the Night Sanitation release button for the last time. There had been many last times. My last Christmas when I'd bought a pack of Gauloises as a treat; my last time in the gym; my last tea; my last exercise. The light in the panel came on Amber. I'd been on fucking amber for weeks. I lay down on the bed and felt powerful, hardly noticed the light shift to green and only just made it out before the entire process aborted. I delivered the two notes under cell doors, couldn't bring myself to look in the spyholes or say anything.

Back in the cell I went to the window for another last time. It was so quiet, light years away from those early days in Brixton and the Scrubs, the all-night shouting from their borstal wings. The last light of the night was squeezed out.

I woke up with the click. The screw said nothing. I got dressed slowly. It was crazy, in an hour I'd be taking it all off again and putting on my own clothes. It was OK, of course it was OK. And I'd done a degree course in that variety of crazy. Down at the recess I ran very hot water and shaved slowly followed by a cold splash for the tingle. After that one last look round the empty cell and down the stairs. Gerry was there, a last minute coincidence, a piece of unexpected parole in his case and we were out on the same day. We grinned at each other, the moody bastard. I'd sworn I'd keep out of his way early mornings, but this time I had a date.

At the control centre there was another wait. It was buzzing with flashing lights, night screws signing off, day screws signing on. The whole thing carrying on as before, who the hell were we, we weren't going to be missed. They'd be unlocked on the wings by now. A soft-toy entrepreneur would be making a grab for my mattress.

We sat down on some steps. The gap between our excitement and official slowness was giving me a pain in the chest. Gerry sorted that out, he demanded his milk ration and I followed suit. Fuck it, we were free men and wandered round the adjacent main kitchen like we were tourists and claimed our milk. Gerry wound up with a white moustache. There was no marmalade involved and we laughed which was like a signal to the screw, like it was him was the Pavlov dog, for him to take us to Reception.

My own clothes, dressing in them, how good that felt. I grinned at myself in the mirror. In the office there were forms to be signed, something about firearms and a sheaf of Social Security stuff. OK, it was all OK, take your time. Then suddenly I was at the door. Such a bland door and next to it the fish-tank visitors had remarked on, like first impressions it was a school they'd come to.

And then I was out. Just like that, as your man says. The immediate car-park in the fields beyond was full of screws' cars. I looked around. My sister was waving in the corner. I walked across and got into her car like it was the most normal thing in the world.

This book would not have been possible without the generosity and enthusiasm of the type designers and foundries who have contributed their amazing glyphs to the project. We would like to extend our greatest thanks and deepest admiration to them all.

A big thank you goes to Sébastien Delobel at Ainsi Fonts, Samuel Carnoky at Carnoky Type, Thierry Blancpain at Grilli Type, Fabian Widmer at Letterwerk, Luzi Gantenbein at Luzi Type, Jeremy Mickel at MCKL Foundry, Clovis Vallois at Nouvelle Noire, Rudy Geeraerts at OurType and Daniela Party at Swiss Typefaces.

A special thank you must also go to Monotype for allowing us to access their gargantuan type library, particularly to Emily Elkins and Allan Haley for their assistance on the project and for advising on the elusive manicule and hedera glyphs.

Published by Cicada Books Limited

Conceived and designed by Adriana Caneva
and Shiro Nishimoto at Off-White (offwhite.co.uk)

Written by Anna Davies

British Library Cataloguing-in-Publication Data.

A CIP record for this book is available
from the British Library.
ISBN: 978-1-908714-28-2

Cicada Books Limited
48 Burghley Road
London
NW5 1UE

T: +44 207 209 2259
E: ziggy@cicadabooks.co.uk
W: www.cicadabooks.co.uk